BUILDING
YOUR
BIBLICAL
STUDIES
LIBRARY

BUILDING YOUR BIBLICAL STUDIES LIBRARY

A Survey of Current Resources

by

Erich H. Kiehl

Publishing House
St. Louis

Copyright © 1988 Concordia Publishing House
3558 S. Jefferson Avenue, St. Louis, MO 63118-3968
Manufactured in the United States of America

Library of Congress Cataloging in Publication Data

Kiehl, Erich H., 1920–
    Building your biblical studies library: survey of current resources/by Erich H. Kiehl.
      p.   cm.
    ISBN 0-570-04489-8 (pbk.): $9.95
    1. Bible—Study—Bibliography. I. TITLE.
Z7770.K53 1988
[BS600.2]   87-38231
016.22—dc19   CIP

1 2 3 4 5 6 7 8 9 10   97 96 95 94 93 92 91 90 89 88

Contents

Preface

The present age is one of a tremendous proliferation of many titles in a wide variety of theological subject areas and topics. These range from very specific studies, such as the development and use of the title "Son of Man," to a very broad overview of the social history of the Old and New Testament worlds.

For anyone working in theology, this is a challenging situation. Many feel the need for some guidance. This is especially true of the student. It is also true of the pastor who seeks to serve his flock faithfully and who properly believes that remaining a careful student of Scripture is an essential part of ministry. One who serves in an institution of theological education feels the same need as he strives to meet his own demanding schedule and to keep informed on pertinent studies for his own personal and professional growth.

Building a library of theological resources is indispensable for one involved in the various areas of kingdom service. To do so with discernment is also a matter of economic necessity. For example, ready access to a source of well-informed, succinct information on the historical development of textual editions of the Old and New Testaments—and their implications for a purposeful study of Scripture in the light of the many English versions—is highly desirable.

This resource seeks to provide such information as well as carefully selected bibliographies covering the subjects arranged in 15 categories. The bibliographies include standard titles in English, especially those that are scholarly and respectful of Scripture. Unfortunately, some valuable resources are no longer in print. In many instances a brief description of the contents is provided to supply additional information.

Valuable assistance, especially in the area of Old Testament studies, was given by Lee Maxwell, a graduate student at Concordia Seminary.

The author prays that this resource will provide useful guidance for growth in knowledge and understanding of God's precious Word.

I

The Text of the Old Testament

A. The Importance of the Qumran Manuscripts

The chance discovery of seven ancient documents in Cave I in 1947 by a bedouin shepherd lad, and the identification of one as a copy of the Book of Isaiah (1QIs^a) and another as a commentary on Habakkuk (1QpHab), led to a flurry of investigations of caves in the immediate area of Qumran and the whole surrounding area. This chance discovery had a profound effect on the knowledge and study of the Old Testament text.

Strangely enough, the initial Qumran texts at first aroused little interest. The Syrian Metropolitan Athanasius Jeshue Samuel had acquired some of the scrolls and consulted a number of scholars, seeking to have them evaluated. Unfortunately, they were skeptical about their authenticity and hence their importance.

Finally in February 1948, he came to the American School of Oriental Research in Jerusalem, where John C. Trever recognized their antiquity. With permission, he photographed parts of the great Isaiah scroll and sent prints to Dr. W. F. Albright at Johns Hopkins University in Baltimore. The latter hailed these as one of the greatest discoveries of modern times. The Isaiah scroll proved to be about 1000 years older than the oldest extant Hebrew copy.

In all, 11 caves were found in the immediate vicinity of Qumran. Among these Cave IV contained the largest number of documents, including thousands of manuscript fragments and about 520 manuscripts. Other caves in the wilderness of Judea and its immediate area were carefully searched. Significant finds discovered somewhat later than those at Qumran were found at Murabba'at, Masada, and Nahal Hever. Copies or fragments of copies of each book of the Old Testament (with the exception of Esther) were found together with a variety of noncanonical texts.

A careful study of the manuscripts through the years has demonstrated that until about the year A.D. 100, there was no single established Hebrew text of the Old Testament in use in Palestine. Rather, there were three distinct Hebrew text-types: the proto-Massoretic, which underlies the text of the Hebrew Scriptures of today; the text which underlies the Septuagint; and the text which is closely related to the Samaritan Pentateuch.

The manuscript of the Book of Numbers found in Cave IV is a mixed text, midway between the Septuagintal and the Samaritan text-types. Also found in Cave IV were three partial manuscripts of the books of Samuel. The oldest (4QSam^b) witnesses to a high-quality text tradition and in many cases is close to the text underlying the Septuagint. Some Greek fragments of the Septuagint were found together with some manuscripts of the Apocrypha and the Old Testament Pseudepigrapha. The Qumran manuscript finds, as well as those at such other sites as Masada, Nahal Hever, and Murabba'at, have given a tremendous impetus to the study of the Old Testament texts and those of noncanonical Jewish literature. This study goes on, and it will shed additional light so important for Biblical studies and for the life, thought-patterns, and the cultural milieu of the late centuries before the coming of Christ and the early centuries of the Christian era.

The Qumran Biblical manuscripts indicate that textual studies seeking to arrive at a standard Hebrew text of the Old Testament had been in process by the Jewish rabbis for some time. It seems that by around A.D. 100 this had been fairly well established. The texts found at Murabba'at inform us that the consonantal base of the Hebrew text was well-fixed by the time of the Bar Kochba revolt in A.D. 132. These also show that the principles for the use of vowel letters had become fixed by that time, even though the process of carrying these out as found in the Hebrew text of today would go on for several centuries.

B. The Old Testament Text

1. History of the Text

The manuscript finds at Qumran and the surrounding area demonstrate that in A.D. 68 there was no single, established text of the Old Testament. Yet a comparison of the fragmentary second Isaiah scroll (1QIs[b]) with that of the first and larger scroll (1QIs[a]) shows that the former followed an archaic and difficult text, which does not differ essentially from the Massoretic text. The second Isaiah scroll dates approximately 100–150 years later than that of the first great Isaiah scroll. However, this later text type was not dominant at Qumran. Rather, the manuscript evidence indicates that there were three dominant text-types in general use in the first century A.D. This is also reflected in the witness of the Old Testament text-types used in the New Testament.

The documents found at Wadi Murabba'at and at Nahal Hever date to ca. A.D. 135. They are all of the general type of the second Isaiah scroll. These second-century documents may properly be termed Proto-Massoretic; they reflect the concern of Rabbi Aqiba (A.D. 55–137) for exacting attention to minute detail. They demonstrate a concern in Judaism for an authoritative text.

This concern for an authoritative text marks a decisive turning point in the history of the text of the Old Testament. Involved in this process were the *sopherim,* the early scholars who wrote out the consonantal text. They are said to have counted all the letters of the text as part of their meticulous care to see to it that the authoritative text was properly transmitted. The work of the Massoretes began in the late fifth century and continued on into the 10th century.

The term "Massorete" means to transmit faithfully the Massorah, the tradition, with extreme care. The Massoretes recorded the traditions by putting notes between the lines of the text and in the margins on both sides as well as at the top and the bottom of the page. Their work also entailed vocalization of the text to assure the proper pronunciation of the Hebrew.

The manuscript finds of the Cairo Geniza (*geniza,* storeroom) shed helpful light on this process, beginning with the fragments from the fifth to the seventh centuries A.D. These documents reflect the process prior to the work of the great Massoretic scholars of the school of Tiberias, which later won out.

2. Editions

From about the last half of the eighth century to the middle of the 10th century, the Ben Asher family was active for five to six generations in the Massoretic work at Tiberias. The manuscripts that survived go back to the activity of the last two members of this illustrious family, that of Moses and of Aaron ben Moses ben Asher. Their textual activity resulted in a complete manuscript of the Old Testament, known as the Aleppo Codex.

The Aleppo Codex was not available for use in the Kittel editions of the *Biblia Hebraica.* Fortunately, the Codex Leningradensis (L) was used, beginning with the third edition of Kittel, completed in 1937. A number of later printings corrected errors and included insertions of variants from the relevant Qumran manuscript finds. According to a colophon, the Codex Leningradensis was copied in A.D. 1008 from exemplars written by Aaron ben Moses ben Asher.

In 1958 the British and Foreign Bible Society in London printed an edition prepared by Norman H. Snaith which drew on the manuscripts of the Ben Asher tradition. The text of this Hebrew Bible is closely related to that of the third edition of Kittel.

Presently the Hebrew University at Jerusalem has in process the publication of a very detailed Hebrew Bible. Parts of this were published in 1965 and in 1975. This edition features an exact reproduction of the Aleppo Codex (ben Asher) and will include the large and the small Massorah. The critical apparatus will also reflect the history of the Old Testament text.

The present standard edition is the *Biblia Hebraica Stuttgartensia,* completed in 1977. This was prepared under the editorship of K. Ellinger and W. Rudolph, together with the assistance (among others) of H. P. Rueger, J. Ziegler, and G. E. Weil. This edition replaces Kittel's *Biblia Hebraica,* last reprinted in 1973.

There is no real difference between the texts of these two editions. However, the advantage of the *Stuttgartensia* is not only its clearer type face but also its revision of Kittel's apparatus and combining the same with the textual notes from Qumran. In the past, these had been positioned at the bottom of the page above the Kittel apparatus. It is important for the student of the Hebrew Bible to be well aware of the text-critical principles involved in both editions, and also to realize that both have some problems. The student should also have a copy of the Septuagint at hand to be able to check out the references made to the Hebrew text.

C. The Samaritan Pentateuch

The Torah became the Scripture of the Samaritan community. Exactly when this happened is a matter of some debate, though it seems to have taken place during the Hasmonean period. Some hold that it came about when John Hyrcanus destroyed the Samaritan temple on Mount Gerizim in 128 B.C. Others suggest that it may have happened somewhat earlier.

The Samaritan Pentateuch is an important witness to a text that once saw widespread use. This is evident from a comparison with some texts found at Qumran, the Septuagint, the New Testament, and also some Jewish texts.

The Samaritan Pentateuch itself probably came into being as a popularized revision of the Hebrew text with the purpose of making the text as intelligible as possible. The Qumran manuscript finds indicate that it was one of the three text-types in use in the first century.

The script of the Samaritan Pentateuch sheds light on the development of the Paleo-Hebrew script. It reflects the full orthography of Hebrew writing of the Hasmonean period. It varies in about 6000 instances from the Massoretic text, and it agrees with the Septuagint around 1900 times against the Massoretic text.

The Samaritan Pentateuch is marked by sectarian readings. After Exodus 20:17, for example, the command was inserted to build a sanctuary on Mount Gerizim (see also Deut. 27:2–3a, 4–7; and 11:30). In Deuteronomy 11:38 the Samaritan Pentateuch reads "beside the oak of Moreh in front of Shechem." In 21 instances in Deuteronomy Samaritan claims with reference to a specific site at which to worship God are included.

Other significant expansions are included to accommodate parallel readings from other parts of the Pentateuch. These reconstruct conversations or record events alluded to elsewhere, such as references to the angel of God visiting Jacob (Gen. 30:36; see 31:11–13); the ongoing contact between God and Pharaoh in Exodus 7:18; 8:4–5, 23; 9:5, 19; 10:2; 11:3; additions to the Ten Commandments after Exodus 20:17, 21 and within verse 19; and also a variety of additions to the Book of Numbers. There are also variations from the Massoretic text in the genealogical records of Genesis 5 and 11.

The oldest known manuscript of the Samaritan Pentateuch is in codex form and is preserved in the library of Cambridge University in England. It contains a date in the middle of the 12th century. Some suggest that it may be older than that.

D. The Septuagint

1. History of Its Text

The Greek translations of the Hebrew text are important sources of information for the text of the Old Testament. Many of the quotations and paraphrases of the Old Testament passages in the New Testament are taken from the Septuagint (LXX), which was so heavily used in the Greek-speaking Jewish dispersion and in the Christian church.

The unknown writer of the Letter of Aristeas, toward the close of the second century B.C., provides an interesting but fictional account of the origin of the LXX. According to him, Ptolemy II Philadelphus (285–247 B.C.) arranged to have the Torah translated into Greek as a worthy addition to the royal library at Alexandria. This involved the labors of 72 men who in 72 days completed a trustworthy translation! The amazed king sent them home to Palestine loaded with valuable gifts.

The anonymous writer of this fictional account was probably an educated member of the Jewish community of Alexandria. He may well have had several purposes in mind: (1) to demonstrate the reliability of the Greek Pentateuch, regarded as a standard text by the Alexandrian Jews; (2) to stress the superiority of the Pentateuch and its wisdom to that of all Greek learning, which was so highly valued and sought after in Alexandria. To do this he drew in part on history in an effort to impress his readers.

The actual translation of the Pentateuch was made in Alexandria because Jews who had settled there needed the Old Testament Scriptures in their new Greek language. The translation of the Pentateuch was probably made sometime between 300–250 B.C. and the rest of the Old Testament sometime thereafter.

The Prolog to the Greek translation of Ecclesiasticus, the Wisdom of Jesus ben Sirach (soon after 132 B.C.), refers to the Greek translation of the Torah and also of "the prophets and the other books." It has been suggested that both the early and the later prophets were completed at the very latest by 200 B.C., and the rest, called "the Writings," soon thereafter. It is probable that the whole Old Testament translation was completed by 180 B.C. at the latest.

The text of the LXX lacks uniformity. The translation of the Pentateuch was the most carefully done. Some have seen at least two translators in the Greek text of Isaiah and the minor prophets. Some books seem to be literal translations and others, such as Job and Daniel, are much more free. The translation of Jeremiah is only seven-eighths as long as that of the Massoretic text, due to the Hebrew text used by the translator. The Qumran finds include a longer text and then a fragmentary text (4QJer[b]) of Jeremiah in Greek. The translation of Samuel is especially helpful because of the poorer state of the Hebrew text.

As time went on and especially because of the Christian use of the LXX, this text-type fell into disfavor among Jews and the Massoretic text won out as a result. This forced the Greek-speaking Jewish communities to find a version to replace that of the LXX.

A disciple of Rabbi Aqiba and a proselyte named Aquila produced a very literal Greek translation of the Hebrew text about A.D. 130. This was cited in a document as having been sanctioned for use in the synagog.

Toward the end of the second century a proselyte named Theodotion revised an existing Greek version, following the Hebrew text. His translation was a more idiomatic Greek than that of Aquila, and it was favorably received by Christians of that period. At about the same time or somewhat later, another version was produced by Symmachus, who had converted to Judaism from Christianity. This version was a more literal translation of the Hebrew but done in good Greek idiom.

The great church father Origen compiled the *Hexapla* sometime in the middle of the third century. His purpose was to bring some order to the confused textual state. He arranged the following texts in six columns: (1) the Massoretic Hebrew text; (2) the Hebrew text transliterated into Greek; followed by the texts (3) of Aquila; (4) of Symmachus; (5) of the LXX; and (6) of Theodotion.

Origen's purpose was to link the LXX to the Hebrew original text as he saw it. He did this especially by using three critical marks in the text of his fifth column to shed light on the relationship between the LXX and the Hebrew text. The church fathers Pamphilus (d. 309) and Eusebius of Caesarea (d. ca. 340) worked to gain recognition for the text of this fifth column as the standard text in Palestine. A second work by Origen is the *Tetrapla,* consisting of the last four columns of the *Hexapla.*

Later recensions of the LXX were made by Hesychius (ca. 300) and Lucian, a presbyter of Antioch (d. 312). According to Jerome, the recension of Hesychius was widely used in Egypt. Lucian's recension gained great respect in Asia Minor and Syria.

Aside from the fragments found at Qumran and Nahal Hever, a variety of other fragments of varying dates of the LXX have been found. Among these are a fragment in the Bodmer Papyri and that of John H. Scheide.

From the period after A.D. 300, complete or almost complete manuscripts of the LXX are extant: Codex Vaticanus (B) and Sinaiticus (S or ‎א‎) dating back to the fourth century; and Codex Alexandrinus (A) and Ephraemi (C) of the fifth century.

Translations were made from the Greek into a variety of European and Oriental languages. Of importance is that of the Old Latin, which goes back to Pope Victor (ca. A.D. 190). The North African church father Tertullian (A.D. ca. 160–ca. 230) popularized this translation through his writings. He and Cyprian (d. A.D. 258) also drew on other Latin translations. These are important since they go back to a Greek text prior to revisions made in the third and fourth centuries. Jerome's Vulgate is also a witness to the attempt to bring order out of the chaotic textual state of the LXX texts.

The Syriac Peshitta is one of the oldest versions of the Old Testament text. It represents the work of many translators. Its origin is shrouded in mystery. Some Jewish translations may underlie some of these translations. The Peshitta translation of Chronicles contains free paraphrases and avoids anthropomorphisms. Another Syriac translation was made early in the seventh century. It follows the text of the LXX column of the *Hexapla.*

After A.D. 300 translations of the LXX were also made in various dialects used by the Coptic church in Egypt, the Ethiopic and the Armenian churches, and also in Arabic.

2. Editions

The 16th century saw the publication of several editions of the LXX. The *Complutensian Polyglot* was planned by Cardinal Ximenes of Spain in 1502 and was carried out by several scholars. The first four volumes presented the Massoretic text, the Vulgate, and the LXX printed in three columns side by side, together with the Aramaic Targum of Onkelos for the Pentateuch at the bottom of the page together with a Latin translation. The last volume carries a date of July 10, 1517. Unfortunately, this polyglot did not receive the sanction of Pope Leo X until March 22, 1520. The set was not published until about 1522. The Old Testament text of this polyglot is of particular value.

The Aldine edition (Venice, 1518) offers a late text of the LXX and is of little value. The Sixtine edition (Rome, 1587) was commissioned by Pope Sixtus V. The text is essentially that of Codex B. Among other later editions, this text was normative for the London Polyglot (1654–57), Holmes and Parsons (1798–1827), Tischendorf (ca. 1850) and the Clarendon Press edition (Oxford, 1875), which serves as the basis for the Hatch and Redpath concordance of the LXX.

More recent critical editions of the LXX include that by H. B. Swete, *The Old Testament in Greek,* in three volumes (1887–91). In 1906 Cambridge University Press began publishing in four volumes an edition edited by Alan E. Brooke, Norman McLean, Henry St. John Thackeray, and others under the title, *The Old Testament in Greek According to the Text of Codex Vaticanus, Supplemented by Other Uncial Manuscripts, with a Critical Apparatus Containing the Variants of the Chief Ancient Authorities for the Text of the Septuagint.* Presently this edition contains the Pentateuch, Joshua, Judges, Ruth, Samuel–Kings, Chronicles, Ezra, Nehemiah, 1 Esdras, Esther, Judith, and Tobit. This resource is also known as "The Larger Cambridge."

It has larger pages and more legible print than the Goettingen edition, which, however, is more up-to-date.

An ongoing project is that of the Goettingen Septuagint under the title, *Septuaginta Vetus Testamentum Graecum auctoritate Societatis Litterarum Goettingensis editum,* scheduled to appear in 16 volumes. Presently about two-thirds of the set has been completed. The purpose of this ongoing series is to print that reading of a text which seems to be best in the light of the manuscript traditions and with proper consideration of the Hebrew text. The apparatus gives the readings of individual textual groups and also of individual manuscripts as they can stand as representatives of groups.

Probably the most commonly used edition of the LXX is Alfred Rahlf's two-volume *Septuaginta, id est, Vetus Testamentum Graece iuxta LXX interpretes,* published by the Wuerttemberg Bible Society in several editions. This is also available in a smaller, single-volume edition. Rahlf's edition is based heavily on the texts of Vaticanus (B), Sinaiticus (S; **א**), and Alexandrinus (A).

3. Characteristics of the LXX

Any translation necessarily involves a certain amount of interpretation. This is discernible in the LXX. The translators lived in a world of different social conditions, customs, thought patterns, and amid a wide variety of pagan beliefs.

Keeping in mind the pagan idols and worship patterns, the translators of the LXX stress the great chasm between the worship of the true God and the non-existent idols so popular in Alexandria and the Greek world. They avoided anthropomorphisms and anthropopathisms. They also sought to place the proper distance between man and God. Thus, in Exodus 19:3 Moses did not go up to God as in the Hebrew text but rather "went up to the mountain of God." They consistently used the Greek *Kurios* for the Hebrew *Yahweh* to stress the universality of God as the Lord of heaven and earth.

At times the LXX text is interpretative, including such matters as how earlier prophecies have been fulfilled. The LXX is not straightforward Greek but rather has many "Hebraic" qualities.

E. Textual Criticism

Although a strictly prescribed method of Old Testament textual criticism has not been worked out, there are basic rules that help one to avoid arbitrariness and subjectivity. Briefly, these may be described as follows:

1. The original reading may be assumed to have been preserved when the Hebrew manuscripts and the versions agree.
2. When the Hebrew manuscripts and versions disagree, either the more difficult reading should be chosen or that which best makes the development of the other reading(s) properly intelligible.
3. Where the Hebrew manuscripts and the versions offer a good reading, and a better reading cannot be demonstrated on the basis of the above rules, the reading of the MT should be permitted to stand.
4. When the Hebrew manuscripts and the versions are different, and none makes proper sense, it is permissible to suggest a reading, but one which should be capable of sensible validation.

F. Selected Bibliography

Biblia Hebraica Stuttgartensia (BHS). Ed. K. Ellinger and W. Rudolf. Stuttgart: Deutsche Bibelstiftung, 1984.

Biblia Hebraica (BHK). Ed. Rudolf Kittel. Stuttgart: Wuerttembergische Bibelanstalt, 1973.

Burrows, Millar, John C. Trever, and William B. Brownlee, eds. *Dead Sea Scrolls of St. Mark's Monastery: The Isaiah Manuscript and the Habakkuk Commentary*. Philadelphia: The American Schools of Oriental Research, 1950.

Cross, Frank M. *The Ancient Library of Qumran and Modern Biblical Studies*. Garden City, NY: Anchor, revised ed., 1981.

Cross, Frank M., and S. Talmon, eds. *Qumran and the History of the Biblical Text*. Cambridge, MS: Harvard University Press, 1975.

Fitzmyer, Joseph P. *The Dead Sea Scrolls: Major Publications and Tools for Study*. Decatur, GA: Scholars Press, 1977. (The latest addendum in 1977.)

Jellicoe, Sidney. *The Septuagint and Modern Study*. Oxford: Clarendon, 1968.

Kahle, Paul. *The Cairo Geniza*. 2nd ed. New York: Praeger, 1959.

Kenyon, F. G. *Our Bible and the Ancient Manuscripts.* Rev. and augmented by A. W. Adams. New York: Harper & Row, 1975.

McCarter, P. Kyle, Jr. *Textual Criticism: Recovering the Text of the Hebrew Bible.* Philadelphia: Fortress, 1986.

Rahlfs, Alfred. *Septuaginta.* 2 vols. in 1. Stuttgart: Deutsche Bibelgesellschaft, 1979.

————. *Septuaginta.* 7th ed. 2 vols. Stuttgart: Wuerttembergische Bibelanstalt, 1962.

Snaith, H. Norman. *Sepher, Torah, Nebiim, and Ketubim.* London: British and Foreign Bible Society, n.d.

Swete, Henry B. *An Introduction to the Old Testament in Greek.* Rev. Richard R. Ottley. New York: KTAV, 1968.

Wonneberger, Reinhart. *Understanding the BHS: A Manual for the Users of the Biblia Hebraica Stuttgartensia.* Tr. Dwight R. Daniels. Rome: Biblical Institute Press, 1984.

Wuerthwein, Ernst. *The Text of the Old Testament: An Introduction to the Biblia Hebraica.* 4th ed. Grand Rapids, MI: Eerdmans, 1979.

II

The Text of the New Testament

A. Early History

All 27 books of the New Testament were written in Greek. Some of the Pauline letters, such as Galatians and 1–2 Thessalonians, were among the earliest written. According to the witness of Irenaeus of Lyon, the apostle John wrote his gospel account while living in Ephesus during the reign of the Emperor Trajan (A.D. 98–117) (*Against Heresies* II.22.5; III.1.1; 3.4).

P[52], the earliest known fragment of the New Testament documents, contains John 18:31–33 on one side and vv. 37–38 on the other. Significant for dating this papyrus is the fact that it was found in a provincial town along the Nile, far removed from Ephesus. This fragment is usually dated at the latest at A.D. 125. This suggests that John's gospel was written by the year A.D. 100.

Just when the books of the New Testament were collected cannot be established. 2 Peter 3:16 gives evidence that the letters of Paul were being collected when this letter was written. Peter refers to them as if they were perfectly familiar to his readers. In his letter to the Corinthians (A.D. 96), Clement of Rome reflects his knowledge of not only Paul's letters to the Corinthians but also of his other letters. Shortly before A.D. 110, Ignatius reminded the Ephesians that Paul remembered them in every letter (*Ephesians* 12:2). The writings of this early church father demonstrate that the gospels, especially Matthew's, were well-known.

Marcion's limited canon, consisting of the heavily edited 10 letters of Paul and the Gospel According to Luke, seemingly aroused the early Christian church in the middle of the second century to begin the process of arriving at the canon of the New Testament. This process assumes an intimate acquaintance of the church with the New Testament writings.

Many handwritten copies of the books of the New Testament were made through the centuries. A formal listing of such extant copies was begun by R. C. Gregory and has been superseded by Kurt Aland. The latest listings indicate that 88 papyri, 274 uncials, 2795 minuscules, and 2209 lectionary manuscripts have been recorded. The oldest is the P^{52} fragment. The uncials date back to the beginning of the fourth century, and the minuscules begin with the ninth century.

By around the second and third centuries, the Greek New Testament had been translated into three key languages of the ancient world: Latin, Syriac, and Coptic. In time, translations were also made into other languages, such as Gothic, Armenian, Ethiopian, Georgian, and Arabic. In the Western world, Latin became the dominant translation.

The earliest copies of the New Testament books are the papyri, beginning with the second century and extending into the eighth century. The most important of these are found in either the Chester Beatty or the Bodmer collections. Interestingly, in the papyri copies of Matthew and John predominate among the gospels. The Book of Acts, Romans, and 1–2 Corinthians are best represented in the papyri of the rest of the New Testament books.

In the papyri the text may be written in capital letters (uncials) or in cursive form (lower case). This is true also of the secular papyri, of which many have been found.

Only two of the uncial manuscripts contain all the books of the New Testament. Two more are nearly complete. Most of the uncial manuscripts were generally formed into groups: the gospels, Acts and the general epistles, the Pauline letters, and the Book of Revelation. Most uncial manuscripts contain at most two of these groups and often only one.

Among the most important uncials are Codex Sinaiticus (ℵ), Vaticanus (B), Alexandrinus (A), Codex Ephraemi Rescriptus (C), Bezae (D), and the Freer Codex (W).

B. Early Printed Editions

The first Greek New Testament was printed some 60 years after Johannes Gutenberg invented printing with movable type. In 1514 Volume 5 of the *Complutensian Polyglot* was printed. This contained the New Testament in Greek together with a Greek glossary with the equivalents in Latin. The other five volumes were printed by July 10, 1517. Unfortunately, the proper sanction by Pope Leo X was not secured until March 22, 1520. The set was not published until 1522.

The first Greek New Testament to be published was prepared by the famous Dutch scholar and humanist Desiderius Erasmus of Rotterdam (1469–1536). He was opportuned by a friend of the publisher, Johann Froben, to prepare copy for publication. For the most part, Erasmus relied on two inferior manuscripts dating from about the 12th century. For the Book of Revelation he had only one copy, which lacked the last six verses. The manuscript itself was often so obscure that he had to translate from the Latin to the Greek. As Erasmus himself later confessed, this edition was "precipitated rather than edited." This first edition was printed by March 1, 1516.

In all, Erasmus published five editions through 1535. These were based on no more than six minuscule manuscripts. The best and the oldest of these agrees with the uncials. But this manuscript he used least, since he considered it an erratic text. In time, Erasmus' editions served as the basis for the *Textus Receptus* (Received Text). His second edition became the basis for Luther's German translation of the New Testament in 1522 and for William Tyndale's translation in 1525.

The second edition of Robert Stephanus, deeply indebted to Erasmus' editions, was reprinted by the famous Elzevir printers in 1533 with the notation: "You have the text, now received by all: in which we give nothing altered nor corrupted." This statement in Latin gave rise to the term *Textus Receptus*.

During the last four centuries, much work has gone into the study of the texts of the Greek New Testament. Among the illustrious scholars who contributed much to the knowledge of the present state of the Greek texts are Theodore Beza (1519–1605), John Mill (1645–1707), Daniel Mace (d. ca. 1753), Johann Albrecht Bengel (1687–1752), Johann Jakob Wettstein (1693–1754), Johann Semler

(1725–91), Johann Jakob Griesbach (1745–1812), Karl Lachmann (1793–1851), Friedrich Constantin von Tischendorf (1815–74), Henry Alford (1818–71), Brooke Foss Westcott (1825–1901), Fenton J. A. Hort (1828–92), Bernhard Weiss (1827–1918), Hermann von Soden (1852–1914), and Eberhard Nestle (1851–1913). To these and many others in the present century students of the Greek New Testament are deeply indebted.

C. Textual Criticism

The student of the Greek New Testament is deeply indebted to Constantin von Tischendorf (1815–74). He searched for, found, and published more manuscripts and also published more critical editions of the Greek texts than anyone else. His eighth edition of the Greek New Testament is the most important, published in two volumes in 1869–72. This included a rich critical apparatus, which contained all the various readings he and his predecessors had found.

In 1881 Brooke Foss Westcott (1825–1901) and Fenton J. A. Hort (1828–92) issued a two-volume Greek New Testament. Included in the introduction were the principles of textual criticism they followed.

Westcott and Hort followed the methodology developed by Griesbach, Lachmann, and other predecessors, and they applied it discerningly. The two major principles involve an analysis of the external and the internal evidence of the textual witnesses. Their edition was truly epochal. The general validity of the Westcott-Hort procedures and principles is still widely acknowledged today, even though additional manuscript finds have required some realignment.

Among others who have made a contribution to the Greek New Testament are Bernhard Weiss (1827–1918) and Hermann von Soden (1852–1914). Weiss adopted those variants that he felt were most appropriate to the author's style and theology. In the process, he came to the conclusion that Codex Vaticanus (B) was the best manuscript. Von Soden's enormous research reflected in his two-part edition (with an extensive prolegomena) remains a monumental work, despite its complexity and shortcomings. The serious textual scholar remains indebted to him.

The widely used Nestle text prepared for the Wuerttembergische Bibelanstalt, Stuttgart, by Eberhard Nestle (and later joined by Kurt Aland) reflects 19th-century scholarship. Since the third edition in 1901, the text was based on a comparison of the texts edited by Tischendorf, Westcott and Hort, and Bernhard Weiss. Nestle printed the reading followed by two of these three texts. His textual apparatus, described as a marvel of condensation, is most useful. It provides a great deal of very accurate textual information, including the witness of many early texts discovered in the present century.

In 1966 the United Bible Societies (UBS) published a new edition, edited by K. Aland, M. Black, B. M. Metzger, and A. Wikgren. These scholars were joined in the second edition by C. Martini. A third, corrected edition has been published and reflects especially the growing witness of the lectionaries. In 1979 the Deutsche Bibelstiftung, Stuttgart, published a parallel edition with the critical apparatus revised by Kurt and Barbara Aland as the 26th edition in the Nestle-Aland series.

In 1971 *A Textual Commentary on the Greek New Testament* was published as a companion to the UBS's third edition. In his introductory comments, Bruce Metzger carefully details the criteria used by the committee in its selections from among variant readings of the manuscripts. This involved a careful, discerning analysis of the external and the internal textual evidence.

The external evidence involves an analysis and evaluation of the date and character of the manuscript witness together with the geographical distribution of the witnesses that support a variant reading. Such evidence takes into account the genealogical relationship of texts and families of manuscripts. It is important to remember that the quality rather than the quantity of the witnesses is crucial.

The internal witness involves the analysis of transcriptional and intrinsic probabilities. Basic to the transcriptional probabilities is the belief that the more difficult reading and, with some exceptions, the shorter reading is normally to be preferred. The intrinsic probabilities depend on considering what the author was more likely to have written. This requires an intimate knowledge of the author's style. In some instances the conflicting evidence may be such as to force the witness of the external evidence to be decisive.

D. The Current State of Textual Criticism

In the past much stress has been laid on the existence of textual families. This has been basic in considering the importance of the external manuscript evidence. This may be summarized thus:

1. The Alexandrian witnesses (e.g., B, ℵ, P[66], P[75]). This family is usually considered the best and most faithful in preserving the original. Brevity and austerity are among the characteristics of this family. The study of the Bodmer papyri P[66] and P[75] indicates that the Alexandrian text-type goes back to an earlier text dated early in the second century.
2. The so-called Western witness (e.g., D, the Old Latin, Old Syriac). This group apparently reflects an uncontrolled tradition of copying and translating. Key characteristics are its use of paraphrase and additions, harmonistic tendencies, and the substitution of synonyms. This is especially reflected in the Book of Acts, which is 10 percent longer in the Western text.
3. The Caesarean witness (P[45], Families 1 and 13). Seemingly dating from the early third century, this textual family is a mixture of Alexandrian and Western readings. Some doubt the certainty of this text-type.
4. The Byzantine witnesses. The latest distinctive text-type is a conflated text, characterized by the attempt of editors to achieve a lucid and complete text with the tendency to combine and harmonize. The Textus Receptus is derived from this textual family. Most of the readings unique to this text are usually recognized as secondary in nature.

Careful study of more recent manuscript finds and of lectionaries has resulted in a variety of approaches. Perhaps the dominant approach is the eclectic. This is divided into the more moderate and the thoroughgoing eclecticism.

The moderate eclecticism is presently most dominant. It consists in weighing the merit of the external evidence versus that of the internal, with the latter's emphasis being on style and scribal activity. Especially in weighing the evidence in some textual problems, the decision made by the practitioner of this approach is based on whether he leans more heavily on the external or the internal evidence. This requires constant vigilance against subjectivity.

The thoroughgoing eclecticism places a heavy emphasis on the internal evidence. This approach seeks to treat each textual reading on its own merit in the light of the various readings, without proper regard for the quality of the manuscripts.

Fortunately, most textual scholars presently hesitate to follow the last approach, with its almost total de-emphasis of external evidence. Most tend to recognize the importance of the Alexandrian text-type (B and ℵ) as the safest guide, especially in difficult and complex readings. This is evident in the text found in the UBS edition of the Greek New Testament.

E. Selected Bibliography

Aland, Kurt, Matthew Black, Carlo M. Martini, Bruce M. Metzger, and Allen Wikgren. *Novum Testamentum Graece.* 26th ed. Stuttgart: Deutsche Bibelstiftung, 1979.

The critical apparatus revised and edited by Kurt and Barbara Aland.

————. *The Greek New Testament.* 3rd corrected ed. New York: United Bible Societies, 1983.

Aland, Kurt and Barbara. *The Text of the New Testament: An Introduction to the Critical Edition and to the Theory and Practice of Modern Textual Criticism.* Tr. Erroll F. Rhodes. Grand Rapids, MI: Eerdmans, 1987.

A companion volume to that of Wuerthwein on the Old Testament text. Takes up the editions from Nestle to the present, the transmission and a description of the manuscripts, an introduction to modern editions, resources, and an introduction to the practice of New Testament criticism, based on 12 basic rules. Includes charts of textual contents of manuscripts and papyri as well as pictures of selected manuscripts.

Finegan, Jack. *Encountering New Testament Manuscripts: A Working Introduction to Textual Criticism.* Grand Rapids, MI: Eerdmans, 1974.

Greenlee, J. Harold. *Introduction to New Testament Textual Criticism.* Grand Rapids, MI: Eerdmans, 1964.

Kenyon, F. G. *The Text of the Greek Bible.* Rev. and augmented by A. W. Adams. 3rd ed. London: Duckworth, 1975.

Metzger, Bruce M. *The Early Versions of the New Testament.* Oxford: Clarendon, 1977.

————. *The Text of the New Testament: Its Transmission, Corruption, and Restoration.* 2nd ed. New York: Oxford, 1968.

————. *A Textual Commentary on the Greek New Testament.* New York: United Bible Societies, 1971.

III

Old Testament Grammars, Lexicons, and Concordances

A. Hebrew Grammars

1. Survey of Development

Soon after 132 B.C. the grandson of Joshua ben Sirach translated his grandfather's Ecclesiasticus, the Wisdom of Jesus, the son of Ben Sirach, from Hebrew into Greek. In his prolog he comments:

> You are urged therefore to read with good will and attention, and to be indulged in cases where, despite our diligent labor in translating, we may seem to have rendered some phrases imperfectly. For what was originally expressed in Hebrew does not have exactly the same sense when translated into another language. (RSV)

The challenge of Biblical interpretation in the Old Testament is to have the Hebrew speak English. This involves a careful, discerning knowledge of the meaning of its vocabulary. It is important to have at least one good grammar and lexicon for this task.

The student of the Biblical text needs to be alert to the order of words in a sentence. This is very true of the Hebrew text. One must remember that the Hebrew verb tenses indicate the kind of action rather than the time of action.

In a sense, a grammar of the Hebrew language gathers diverse strands of learning and culture through the ages. The following merit special mention in a quick survey of the development of the Hebrew grammar.

Aaron ben Asher of the 10th century served as the connecting link between the Massoretes and grammarians. Saadia ben Joseph (889–942), the head of the Academy of Sura, was the first to establish a Hebrew grammar, distinct from the Massoretes. His explanation of Hebrew forms is still a feature of a good Hebrew grammar.

Abraham Ibn Izra (ca. 1092–1167) was the first to present grammatical features with reference to the Old Testament. David ben Joseph Kimchi (Kimhi; 1167?–1235?) developed a grammar, lexicon, and commentaries and thereby made a tremendous contribution to a more scientific study of the Hebrew. His work had an enormous affect on the Christian scholars of the Reformation, who understood that the study of Hebrew was essential for Biblical interpretation.

In 1506 Johannes Reuchlin (1455–1522) published his most important work, *De Rudimentis Hebraicis,* a Hebrew lexicon and grammar. Gesenius called Reuchlin "the father of Hebrew philology among the Christians." Reuchlin taught Melanchthon, Luther's associate. Through the years other scholars, such as Albert Schultens (1686–1750), firmly established the method of a comparative grammar.

Heinrich Friedrich Wilhelm Gesenius (1786–1842) ushered in a new era of Semitic studies. He issued the earliest edition of his *Hebraisch-deutsches Handworterbuch ueber Schriften des Alten Testaments* in two volumes in 1810–12. This was followed in 1813 by the first edition of his Hebrew grammar. This and a work published in 1817 set the pattern for subsequent editions known as the Gesenius' grammar.

In 1881 Emil Kautzsch published a thoroughly revised 23rd edition of the grammar. The *Gesenius Hebrew Grammar,* considered by many to be the best reference grammar, was translated by Arthur E. Cowley from the 26th German edition and corrected by the 28th German edition (Oxford: Clarendon, 2nd ed., 1910) and is presently in its 15th printing (1980).

Another outstanding name in the area of Hebrew grammar is Georg Heinrich August Ewald (1803–75). James Kennedy translated the syntax part of Ewald's grammar and published it in 1879 (Edinburgh: T. & T. Clark). Full indexes for references add to the value of this work. Also in the tradition of Ewald is A. B. Davidson's *Hebrew*

Syntax (Edinburgh: T. & T. Clark, 3rd ed., reprinted 1924), as well as Davidson's *An Introductory Hebrew Grammar* (Edinburgh: T. & T. Clark, 1880). This was revised by J. E. McFadyen in 1916.

2. The Present Situation

Although the evaluation of grammars currently in use may vary somewhat from one scholar to the other, the following titles are among those in current use.

The usual reference grammar today is still that of Gesenius' *Hebrew Grammar* discussed above. Similar to H. G. Nunn's *A Short Syntax of New Testament Greek* on a smaller scale is Ronald Williams' *Hebrew Syntax* (University of Toronto Press, 1976).

For use in beginning and for review purposes. the following deserve mention:

Weingreen, Jacob. *Practical Grammar for Classical Hebrew*. 2nd ed. Oxford: Clarendon, 1959.

The exercises are Biblical and the paradigms in the back provide quick and easy reference.

Lambdin, Thomas O. *An Introduction to Biblical Hebrew*. New York: Scribners, 1971.

Like Weingreen, this is primarily a teaching text and assumes some knowledge of Semitic language. It is also written at a higher level. It is more philologically up-to-date than Weingreen.

Mansoor, Menahem. *Biblical Hebrew Step by Step*. Grand Rapids, MI: Baker, 1978.

Unfortunately this text does not advance beyond the Qal system.

Sperber, Alexander. *A Historical Grammar of Biblical Hebrew*. Leiden: Brill, 1966.

Sperber draws on a wide collection of examples of grammar from the Hebrew Bible. He also suggests solutions to many grammatical problems.

Waltke, Bruce. *An Intermediate Hebrew Grammar*. Winona Lake: Eisenbrauns, 1984.

Williams, Ronald J. *Hebrew Syntax: An Outline.* Toronto: University of Toronto Press, 1967.

B. Hebrew Lexicons

From 1810 to 1812 Wilhelm Gesenius published a two-volume *Hebraisch-deutsches Handworterbuch ueber die Schriften des Alten Testaments*. This went through several enlargements and revisions. Translation into the English language was undertaken by Edward Robinson and published in 1836 with a later revision in 1854. Another translation was published by Samuel Prideaux Tregelles in 1847.

The latest translation is that edited by Francis Brown, Samuel R. Driver, and Charles A. Briggs and published in 1907 under the title *A Hebrew and English Lexicon of the Old Testament* (BDB). The last reprint was made in 1966. This is still a standard resource.

This lexicon lacks information from Ugaritic and other linguistic finds. It also reflects the evolutionary view of religion and the documentary hypothesis in vogue in Britain when this translation was made. This resource restricts the variations in meanings of words and also relies too heavily on etymology. It tends to treat verbal conjugations as if each had a relatively fixed meaning. All this is due to the fact that it reflects the state of scholarship in the early 20th century.

A very helpful supplementary tool for use with this lexicon is *Index to Brown, Driver & Briggs Hebrew Lexicon,* compiled by Bruce Einspahr (Chicago: Moody, rev. ed., 1977). The listing of Hebrew words begins with Genesis 1 and continues through Malachi. An addenda in the same order supplements the listing.

A more recent lexicon than BDB is that of Ludwig Koehler and Walter Baumgartner, *Lexicon in Veteris Testamenti Libros* (Leiden: Brill, 2nd ed., 1958). This lexicon is based on the third edition of Kittel's *Biblia Hebraica*. Definitions are given in both German and English. This lexicon provides new information, including also Ugaritic and the Qumran finds.

Based on the second edition of Koehler-Baumgartner and on two-thirds of the third edition is the work of William Holladay, *A Concise Hebrew and Aramaic Lexicon of the Old Testament* (Grand Rapids, MI: Eerdmans, 1971). Although it is much more up-to-date and very reliable, it does not contain the useful and detailed references to cognates in other Semitic languages found in both BDB and Koehler-Baumgartner.

Recent years have seen the release of three of four projected volumes of *A Reader's Hebrew-English Lexicon of the Old Testament* by Terry A. Armstrong, Douglas L. Busby, and Cyril F. Carr. Volume I contains words found in Genesis–Deuteronomy, Volume II those of Joshua–2 Kings, and Volume III those of Isaiah–Malachi. The first two volumes have been combined in a single volume by Zondervan. The final volume is scheduled for later release.

This lexicon lists all the words that occur 50 times or less, verse by verse, in the order of their occurrence. Those occurring more than 50 times are listed in the appendix. Definitions are based on BDB but have been checked for meaning within the context of the text. Included also is their frequency of use in a given book and in the Old Testament. The purpose of the book is to enhance a purposeful study and understanding of the Hebrew Old Testament.

C. Concordances

A concordance is a valuable tool in Biblical studies, for it lists the places in Scripture where a given word is found. A proper use of a concordance is helpful to determine the usage, distribution, and the contexts in which a given word is found.

For many years the standard work has been Solomon Mandelkern's *Veteris Testamenti Concordantiae Hebraicae atque Chaldaicae* (Jerusalem: Schocken, 8th ed., 1969). It is written only in Hebrew and Latin and lists words in a somewhat complicated order. The words are classified in almost every conceivable manner.

Less complicated and somewhat easier to use is the concordance by Gerhard Lisowsky and Leonhard Rost, *Konkordanz zum hebraeischen Alten Testament* (Stuttgart: Wurttembergische Bibelanstalt, 1958). The Hebrew is hand-written, with vowel pointings. The emphasis is on nouns and verbs. It is less complete than Mandelkern.

A very useful concordance is that by George V. Wigram, *The Englishman's Hebrew and Chaldee Concordance of the Old Testament* (Grand Rapids, MI: Zondervan, 3rd ed., reprint, 1978). It lists every occurrence of a Hebrew word with the passage quoted in English, the key word being in italics. It also provides a list of the different English words used to translate a Hebrew word, as well as the various Hebrew words translated by the same word in English.

A recent publication is *A New Concordance of the Old Testament* by Abraham Even-Shoshan (Jerusalem, 1983). This resource is easier to use than Mandelkern or Lisowsky. Terms are listed alphabetically, the verb forms under root. It does have disadvantages: it uses a number code system; the citations use Hebrew names of the books and Hebrew number-letters for the chapters; abbreviations are in Hebrew; the base text is the Koren, not that of Kittel or the Stuttgart edition. A key comes with the book to assist in decoding some of its unique features.

Not to be overlooked for such information is Robert Young's *Analytical Concordance to the Bible* (Nashville: Nelson, rev. ed., 1980). This work lists the Hebrew and/or the Greek word equivalent for each entry in the heading of each English word and then lists the passage where this word is used. *Strong's Exhaustive Concordance of the Bible,* by James Strong (Nashville: Nelson, 1982) gives the Hebrew in transliterated form.

D. The Septuagint

The standard introduction to the Septuagint is Henry Barclay Swete's *An Introduction to the Old Testament in Greek* (New York: KTAV, rev. ed. by Richard R. Ottley, 1914, 1968). Richard R. Ottley's *A Handbook to the Septuagint* (London: Methuen, 1920) provides a more comprehensive introduction. Sidney Jellicoe's *The Septuagint and Modern Study* (Oxford: Clarendon, 1968; Eisenbraun reprint, 1978) surveys the more recent Septuagint studies.

Henry St. John Thackeray began writing *A Grammar of the Old Testament in Greek* (Cambridge, 1909) but unfortunately completed only the first volume, "Introduction, Orthography, and Accidence."

Because of a lack of such reference material, it is necessary to draw on the resources of inclusive grammars of the New Testament. The most comprehensive for such a purpose is F. W. Blass and A. Debrunner, *A Grammar of New Testament and Other Early Christian Literature,* translated and revised by Robert W. Funk (University of Chicago, 1961). Also helpful because of its wide range of Koine Greek is Volume I *Prolegomena,* Chapters 1–3, of *A Grammar of New Testament Greek* by James Hope Moulton (Edinburgh: T. & T. Clark, 3rd. ed., 1908).

In 1980 the grammar of the 1905 edition of *Selections from the Septuagint* by F. C. Conybeare and St. George Stock was reprinted under the title *A Grammar of Septuagint Greek* (Grand Rapids, MI: Zondervan). For many years this was the standard grammar of the LXX. It presents the grammar in a careful, succinct form.

Among other helpful studies for Septuagintal grammar is A. T. Robertson's *A Grammar of the Greek New Testament in the Light of Historical Research* (Nashville: Broadman, 1923). The grammatical and textual criticism references in *The Text of the Septuagint: Its Corruptions and Their Emendations* by Peter Walters (formerly Katz) edited by D. W. Gooding (Cambridge, 1973) are also helpful.

Works that may be helpful as an introduction to the language of the Septuagint are James Barr's *The Semantics of Biblical Language* (Oxford University Press, 1961), E. C. Colwell's "The Greek Language" in *The Interpreter's Dictionary of the Bible,* Volume II, (Nashville: Abingdon, 1962), and Nigel Turner's "The Unique Character of Biblical Greek," in *Vetus Testamentum* (Vol. 5, 1955; pp. 203–13).

Presently there is no lexicon of the Septuagint. The best resources available are Walter Bauer, *A Greek-English Lexicon of the New Testament and Other Early Christian Literature,* edited by W. F. Arndt, F. W. Gingrich, and F. W. Danker (University of Chicago Press, 2nd ed., 1979), and Henry G. Liddell and Robert Scott, *A Greek-English Lexicon* (with supplement; Oxford: Clarendon, 1968). Broader in scope than Bauer-Arndt-Gingrich-Danker and less bulky than the larger Liddell-Scott is Henry G. Liddell and Robert Scott's *An Intermediate Greek-English Lexicon* (Oxford: Clarendon, 1889; 1978 printing).

Not to be overlooked is *The Vocabulary of the Greek Testament Illustrated from the Papyri and Other Non-Literary Sources* by James Hope Moulton and George Milligan (London: Hodder and Stoughton, 1952).

The standard concordance is that by Edwin Hatch and Henry A. Redpath, *A Concordance to the Septuagint and the Other Greek Versions of the Old Testament (Including the Apocryphal Books)* (Graz: Akademische Druck & Verlagsanstalt, 3rd ed., 2 vols., 1955). This gives the Hebrew word(s) that a particular term is used to translate. It also has an index of Hebrew words and gives the various Greek words that are used from the Hebrew.

A complete concordance for the Apocrypha has been published: Lester T. Whitelock, ed., *An Analytical Concordance of the Books of the Apocrypha* (University Press of America, 1978).

E. Cognate Languages

Discoveries in the more recent years have especially underlined the importance of comparative philology. The following selected titles will prove helpful to the Biblical scholar:

Bergstraesser, Gotthelf. *Introduction to the Semitic Languages: Text Specimens and Grammatical Sketches.* English trans. with notes, bibliography, and appendix by Peter T. Daniels. Winona Lake: Eisenbrauns, 1983.

Rosenthal, Franz. *A Grammar of Biblical Aramaic.* Wiesbaden: Otto Harrassowitz, 1961.
  This rather comprehensive text presents data from the Aramaic through the end of the Persian Empire in 333 B.C.

Gordon, Cyrus H. *Ugaritic Textbook.* Rome: Pontifical Biblical Institute, 1965.

Fitzmyer, Joseph A., and Daniel J. Harrington. *A Manual of Palestinian Aramaic Texts: Second Century B.C.–Second Century A.D.* Rome: Biblical Institute Press, 1978.

Harris, Zellig S. *A Grammar of the Phoenician Language.* New Haven: American Oriental Society, 1952.

Segert, Stanislav. *A Grammar of Phoenician and Punic.* Munich: C. H. Beck, 1976.

F. Theological Dictionaries

The *Theological Dictionary of the New Testament,* edited by Gerhard Kittel and Gerhard Friedrich, includes the Hebrew antecedents of the Greek terms included in this set. Two other titles have appeared with specific reference to the Old Testament.

Botterweck, G. Johannes, and Helmer Ringgren, eds. *Theological Dictionary of the Old Testament.* Grand Rapids: Eerdmans, I, 1974; II, 1975; III, 1978; IV, 1980; V, 1985.
  Additional volumes to complete this set will appear from time to time. This has been described as the "Kittel" of the Old Testament.

Harris, R. Laird, Gleason L. Archer, and Bruce K. Waltke, eds. *Theo-*

logical Wordbook of the Old Testament. 2 vols. Chicago: Moody, 1980.

More concise than Botterweck-Ringgren, these volumes make much use of the latest linguistic evidence. Entries are given in Hebrew and English transliteration.

IV

New Testament Grammars, Lexicons, and Concordances

A. Grammars

1. Survey of Development

In 1822 Georg Winer (1789–1858) published the first scientific grammar of the language of the New Testament under the title *Grammatik des neutestamentlichen Sprachidiom* (Leipzig). Contrary to the prevailing view that the language of the Greek New Testament must be seen in terms either of the Hebrew syntax or of classical Greek, Winer demonstrated that the Greek New Testament must be studied on its own terms in accordance with rational philology. His grammars went through eight German and five English editions.

The first person to note and point out the intrinsic relationship between the Koine and New Testament Greek was Adolf Deissmann (1866–1937). While leafing through a publication of transcriptions of papyri at Berlin, he was struck by the similarity between the papyri and the Greek of the New Testament.

This startling discovery launched him on a lifetime of study, resulting in especially two series of publications: *Bible Studies* and *Light from the Ancient Past*. The former, translated from German into English by Alexander Grieve, was published by T. & T. Clark in 1901 and 1909. The second title was translated by L. P. M. Strahan and first published by T. & T. Clark in 1910, and it was reprinted by Baker Book House in 1980. Deissmann demonstrated the rich rewards of giving careful attention to the vocabulary and the syntax of the papyri for a better understanding of the Greek New Testament.

The work of Winer and Deissmann stimulated James Hope Milligan to publish in 1906 Volume I, *Prolegomena,* of what is today a four-volume work under the title *A Grammar of the New Testament Greek* (Edinburgh: T. & T. Clark). Moulton had a flair for making grammar both authoritative and interesting. W. F. Howard published the second volume *Accidence and Word-Formation* (1929). Nigel Turner published the last two volumes of the series: Volume III *Syntax* (1963) and Volume IV *Style* (1976). Turner reflects a different perspective than Moulton.

In 1914 the first of five editions of A. T. Robertson's *A Grammar of the Greek New Testament in the Light of Historical Research* was published. This is a comprehensive treatment of the various aspects of the grammar of the Greek New Testament. Some of his positions reflect the thinking of his time. The language is also somewhat wordy and cumbersome. The fourth edition was republished by Broadman Press in 1947.

The most recent and perhaps the best descriptive grammar is that by Friedrich Blass, *Grammatik des neutestamentlichen Griechisch,* first published in 1896. This was oriented toward classical Greek as a norm. Albert Debrunner reworked a later edition to reflect the increasing amount of information available as a result of the study of the papyri. His work was published as the sixth edition in 1931. Robert W. Funk revised the ninth edition and translated it into English. This was published in 1961. Unfortunately, the revision does not adequately rework the different emphases of Blass and Debrunner. A fully revised German edition was published in 1984 by Friedrich Rehkopf under the title *Grammatik des neutestamentlichen Griechisch* (Goettingen: Vandenhoeck und Ruprecht, 16th rev. ed.).

The Funk-Blass-Debrunner grammar makes a liberal use of the Septuagint. It quotes the manuscripts where differing readings make a given text difficult to ascertain. The apostolic fathers are also cited frequently.

2. Advanced Grammars

The following are advanced grammars of the Greek New Testament:

Blass, Friedrich, and Albert Debrunner. *A Greek Grammar of the New Testament and Other Early Christian Literature.* Trans. and rev. Robert W. Funk. Chicago: University of Chicago Press, 1961.

Moulton, James H., and W. F. Howard. *A Grammar of New Testament Greek* (Edinburgh: T. & T. Clark): Vol. I, *Prolegomena,* by Moulton, 3rd ed., 1908; Vol. II, *Accidence and Word-Formation,* by Moulton and Howard, 1929; Vol. III, *Syntax,* by Nigel Turner, 1963; Vol. IV, *Style,* by Turner, 1976.

Robertson, A. T., *A Grammar of the Greek New Testament in the Light of Historical Research.* 4th ed. Nashville: Broadman, 1947.

3. Intermediate Grammars and Study Helps

Beekmann, John, and John Callow. *Translating the Word of God.* Grand Rapids, MI: Zondervan, 1974.
Stress on the importance of the analysis of genitives on the basis of linguistics.

Burton, Ernest DeWitt. *Syntax of the Moods and Tenses in New Testament Greek.* 3rd ed. Edinburgh: T. & T. Clark, 1898.
Very helpful for a careful analysis of Greek verbs.

Funk, Robert W. *A Beginning-Intermediate Grammar of Hellenistic Greek.* 2nd ed. 3 vols. Atlanta: Scholars Press, 1973.

Hanna, Robert. *A Grammatical Aid to the Greek New Testament.* Grand Rapids, MI: Baker, 1983.
Following the canonical order of the books of the New Testament, grammatical comments are keyed to standard grammars and grammatical helps.

Moule, C. F. D. *An Idiom Book of New Testament Greek.* 2nd ed. Cambridge: Cambridge University Press, 1963.
An extremely useful book providing many helpful insights.

Nunn, H. P. V. *A Short Syntax of New Testament Greek.* 5th ed. Cambridge: Cambridge University Press, 1931.
Excellent in arrangement and discussion of syntax, this is especially valuable as a quick review resource.

Robertson, A. T., and William Hershey Davis. *New Short Grammar of the Greek New Testament.* 10th ed. Grand Rapids, MI: Baker, 1977.

Rienecker, Fritz. *A Linguistic Key to the Greek New Testament.* Trans. with additions and revisions by Cleon L. Rogers, Jr. Grand Rapids, MI: Zondervan, 1980.

Contains a wide range of information on grammar, points of history, and interpretation in succinct form.

Turner, Nigel. *Grammatical Insights into the New Testament.* Edinburgh: T. & T. Clark, 1977.

Provides much information on selected texts.

Wuest, Kenneth. *The Practical Use of the Greek Testament.* Rev. Donald Wise. Chicago: Moody, 1982.

Zerwick, Max, and Mary Grosvener. *A Grammatical Analysis of the Greek New Testament.* 3rd ed. Rome: Biblical Institute, 1981.

Zerwick, Max. *Biblical Greek: Illustrated by Examples.* Trans. Joseph Smith and adapted from 4th Latin ed. Rome: Pontifical Institute, 1963.

Both titles by Zerwick are very helpful resources with much valuable information on grammar and language in succinct form.

4. Beginning Grammars

Kaufman, Paul L. *An Introductory Grammar of New Testament Greek.* Palm Springs, CA: Ronald N. Haynes, 1982.

Machen, J. Gresham. *New Testament Greek for Beginners.* New York: Macmillan, 1923.

Well-suited also for private instruction.

Voelz, James. *Fundamental Greek Grammar.* St. Louis: Concordia, 1985.

Wenham, J. W. *Key to Elements of the New Testament Greek.* New York: Cambridge, 1965.

Accent marks are omitted.

Whittaker, Molly. *New Testament Greek: An Introduction.* Rev. ed. London: SCM Press, 1980. Supplementary booklet: *New Testament Greek Grammar: Key to Exercises* (1969).

Needs to be used in a classroom setting by a skilled teacher.

B. Lexicons

1. The Development of New Testament Greek Lexicons

A lexicon is basically a guide to the meaning of words. Its function is to help a reader through a study of the various forms and meanings of words to arrive at the true meaning of a word as used in a given context. In some instances words may be used interchangeably. The proper use of a lexicon will show why in certain cases one word or synonym may be used properly and in another instance may not.

The first Greek New Testament lexicon with scholarly pretensions was that of Georg Pasor's *Lexicon Graeco-Latinum in Novum Testamentum* published in 1619. He listed words alphabetically according to word roots. In another edition he attempted to remedy the disadvantage of this approach. A later lexicographer began in 1640 the practice of listing all words in alphabetical order.

Adolf Deissmann's discovery of the importance of the papyri for New Testament studies left its decisive impact on the lexicography of the New Testament. Deissmann's findings inspired James Hope Moulton and George Milligan to begin work on *The Vocabulary of the Greek Testament, Illustrated from the Papyri and Other Non-literary Sources*. The first part appeared in 1914 and the second in 1915. The whole work as a single volume was published in 1930.

This resource offers a mass of material on Koine Greek in use before, during, and after the New Testament era. The papyri and their vocabulary shed much light on life in that era and its terminology in context. It is a very valuable resource for the student of the New Testament.

Upon the death of Erwin Preuschen, Walter Bauer of Goettingen undertook to revise the former's Greek-German lexicon of 1910. His revision appeared in 1920 and a third revised edition was issued in 1937.

In preparation for the fourth edition, Bauer made a systematic search in Greek literature up to the Byzantine era for parallels to the language of the Greek New Testament. This edition was revised and augmented in English by William F. Arndt and F. Wilbur Gingrich. It was published by the presses of both the University of

Chicago and Cambridge University in England. A second edition appeared in 1979, based on Bauer's fifth edition of 1958 and revised and augmented by Frederick W. Danker and F. Wilbur Gingrich. This was published by the University of Chicago Press.

C. Lexicons and Lexicographical Aids

Bauer, Walter. *A Greek-English Lexicon of the New Testament and Other Early Christian Literature.* Ed. W. F. Arndt, F. W. Gingrich, F. W. Danker. 2nd ed. Chicago: University of Chicago Press, 1979.

Alsop, John R., ed. *An Index to the Revised Bauer-Arndt-Gingrich Greek Lexicon.* Second ed. by F. Wilbur Gingrich and Frederick W. Danker. Grand Rapids, MI: Zondervan, 1981.

Abbot-Smith, George, ed. *A Manual Greek Lexicon of the New Testament.* Edinburgh: T. & T. Clark, 1936.

Gingrich F. W. *Shorter Lexicon of the Greek New Testament.* Chicago: University of Chicago Press, 1965.

Kubo, Sakae. *A Reader's Greek-English Lexicon of the New Testament and a Beginner's Guide for the Translation of New Testament Greek.* Grand Rapids, MI: Zondervan, 1975.

Lampe, Geoffrey. *Patristic Greek-Lexicon.* Oxford: Clarendon, 1961–68.

Liddell, H. G., and R. Scott. *A Greek-English Lexicon.* 9th ed. 2 vols. Rev. H. S. Jones and R. McKenzie. Oxford: Clarendon, 1949.

Moulton, Harold K., ed. *The Analytical Greek Lexicon Revised.* Grand Rapids, MI: Zondervan, 1978.

Moulton, J. H., and G. Milligan. *The Vocabulary of the Greek Testament Illustrated from the Papyri and Other Non-literary Sources.* London: Hodder & Stoughton, 1952; reprinted by Eerdmans, 1974.

Souter, Alexander. *The Pocket Lexicon to the Greek New Testament.* Oxford: Clarendon, 1929.

D. Theological Dictionaries

In 1927 Gerhard Kittel of Tuebingen together with a group of German New Testament scholars began the monumental task of writing a comprehensive theological dictionary. The first volume appeared in 1933 and the final volume in 1973. At Kittel's death in 1948,

Gerhard Friedrich assumed the editorship of Volumes V (1954) through IX (1973). These volumes increasingly reflect modern research and a greater commitment to tradition-historical criticism. The English translation was ably done by Geoffrey W. Bromiley together with the 10th index volume compiled under his direction.

In *The Semantics of Biblical Language* (Oxford: Clarendon, 1961) James Barr questioned the philological approach taken in the above set with its overemphasis on etymology and its implications. The preface to Volume IX by G. Friedrich demonstrates that the criticism was heard. Etymological discussion was reduced considerably after 1961. Closer attention was paid to the context in which given words were used in the text. Incidentally, Moises Silva has written a very helpful work, *Biblical Words and Their Meaning: An Interpretation of Lexical Semantics* (Grand Rapids, MI: Zondervan, 1983).

In the summer of 1985 Eerdmans published a single-volume abridgment of this nine-volume set prepared by Geoffrey Bromiley. The mass of material was reduced to around one-sixth, or around 1375 pages. The focus of this one-volume condensation is on the Biblical and especially the New Testament usage with emphasis on the theological meaning. The Greek is transliterated. The articles are keyed to the original volume and page numbers.

In 1965 the first fascicle of *Theologisches Begriffslexikon zum Neuen Testament* (Wuppertal: Theologischer Verlag Rolf Brockhaus) appeared under the editorship of Lothar Coenen, Erich Beyreuther, and Hans Bietendorf. The completed work was translated with additions and revisions with Colin Brown serving as the general editor. It was published in 1975 in three volumes under the title *The New International Dictionary of New Testament Theology*. A helpful feature is its extensive bibliography in both English and in the languages of the Continent.

This resource groups words under related ideas. The stress is on a concise discussion of the use and meaning of key words in the New Testament against their background both in the world of that time and in the Old Testament.

Kittel, Gerhard, and Gerhard Friedrich, eds. *Theological Dictionary of the New Testament*. Trans. Geoffrey Bromiley. 10 vols. including index. Grand Rapids, MI: Eerdmans, 1964–76.

Bromiley, Geoffrey. *Theological Dictionary of the New Testament.* An abridgment of TDNT cited above, ed. Gerhard Kittel and Gerhard Friedrich. Grand Rapids, MI: Eerdmans, 1985.

Brown, Colin, ed. *The New International Dictionary of New Testament Theology.* 3 vols. Grand Rapids, MI: Zondervan, 1975–78.

E. Concordances

A concordance serves a variety of purposes. It may be used to determine more surely the true meaning of a word or to see how its meaning is enriched in its use in various passages and contexts. A concordance is helpful to study distinctive truths of Scripture or to learn all that may be learned about the life and activity of a given character. A proper use of a concordance is important for the theological contribution it can make. This is especially true of its use to gain a better understanding of the Greek New Testament. The following is a list of recent and older concordances.

Bachmann H., and H. Slaby, eds. *Computer-Konkordanz zum Novum Testamentum Graece von Nestle-Aland, 26 Auflage, und zum Greek New Testament, 3rd ed.* Berlin: Walter de Gruyter, 1980.

Moulton, William, and A. S. Geden. *A Concordance to the Greek Testament According to the Texts of Westcott and Hort, Tischendorf and the English Revisers.* 5th ed. Rev. and ed. H. K. Moulton. Edinburgh: T. & T. Clark, 1978.

Schmoller, Otto, ed. *Handkonkordanz zum griechischen Neuen Testament.* Based on Nestle. Stuttgart: Privilegierte Wuerttembergische Bibelanstalt, 1949.

Wigram, George V. *The Englishman's Greek Concordance of the New Testament.* 9th ed. Grand Rapids, MI: Zondervan, 1970.

V

English Versions of the Bible

A. Early Versions

For many years the Latin Vulgate was the standard version used in the West in both church and school. This restricted the reading of Scripture and also much of the understanding to those who could read and understand Latin.

In what is today the English-speaking world, several attempts were made to translate parts of the Bible into the Anglo-Saxon language, sometimes termed "Old English." These attempts include the Lindisfarne Gospels by Eadfrith (ca. 696–698); the psalms translated by Aldhelm, the bishop of Sherborne; the work of the Venerable Bede who translated part of the Gospel According to John before his death in 735; and also parts of the Old Testament translated by Abbot Aelfric (ca. 955–ca. 1020). Some Anglo-Saxon versions of the gospels, the psalms, and other parts of the Old Testament have also come down to us.

The Anglo-Saxon period ended soon after the Norman conquest in 1066, when the language was much affected by the language of the invaders. The resulting change in language is sometimes referred to as "Middle English."

John Wycliffe (ca. 1330–84) felt that the common people needed to have the Scriptures in their own language so that they could better understand its meaning and importance for their faith and life. For him the Scriptures were the absolute authority in matters of faith and life. He himself is regarded as the translator of the New Testament. The Old Testament was done by his follower Nicholas of Hereford. This was completed in 1382. This rather literal and difficult translation was revised into a more idiomatic Middle English by John Purvey, a follower of Wycliffe.

B. Tyndale and His Influence

It must be remembered that prior to the invention of the printing press, everything had to be written by hand. The invention of the printing press and especially, somewhat later, the invention of movable type by Johannes Gutenberg (ca. 1450) gave impetus to Bible translations. The revival of learning promoted the knowledge of Greek and Hebrew and the study of available manuscripts of the Bible. Luther's Ninety-Five Theses and consequent developments of the Reformation gave great impetus to translating the Bible into vernacular languages.

In his preface to the first edition of the Greek New Testament, Erasmus issued a call for versions of the Bible in the languages of the common people. This was echoed by both Luther and Tyndale. By 1521 Luther had published his German translation of the New Testament. By 1534 the whole Bible, including the Apocrypha, had appeared.

As a comparison of the two demonstrates, William Tyndale benefited from having a copy of Luther's translation of the New Testament. Tyndale's translation of the New Testament began to be printed in 1525 and appeared in 1526. Before his arrest and martyr's death, he translated the Pentateuch, Genesis, and Jonah and revised his New Testament translation and also that of Genesis.

Tyndale's translation of the New Testament left a profound impact on all of the English revisions for almost four centuries. This includes the American Standard Version of 1901. What is sometimes termed "Bible language" goes back to the work of Tyndale. Much of the King James Version reads as Tyndale had rendered it. The translations from the time of Wycliffe through the King James Version to the American Standard depend on each other.

At a conference of all religious groups at Hampton Court in 1604, it was proposed by Dr. John Reynolds, President of Corpus Christi College, Oxford, that a new translation be prepared. King James I enthusiastically accepted the proposal.

The 47 translators included most of the leading classical and

Oriental scholars in England. They had ready access to all existing translations, both English and foreign, as well as the Latin, the Syriac Peshitta, and the Targums. For the New Testament the translators used Erasmus' editions of 1516 and 1522, based on late manuscripts.

In the preface, the translators stated that their concern was not "to make a new translation, nor yet to make of a bad one a good one ... but to make a good one better, or out of many good ones one principal good one, not justly to be excepted against." Great care was taken to avoid biases of sectarian theology. The translators phrased their translation in the exquisite prose of their age, the age of Shakespeare.

Some additions, such as Ussher's chronology, were added from time to time. Revisions of the translation were made in 1762 and again by Dr. Blayney of Oxford in 1769. Basically this last revision is known today as the King James Version.

In the ensuing years came the discovery of older and better manuscripts than those on which the King James Version is based. The study of these, and especially Tischendorf's discovery of Codex Sinaiticus in 1859, highlighted the need for a revision. A group of scholars appointed by the Church of England revised and published a revision of the New Testament in 1881 and the Old Testament in 1885. This revision became known as the Revised Version. An American team published its revision in 1901, and this became known as the American Standard.

C. Recent Translations

The 20th century has witnessed the appearance of a variety of revisions, new translations, and paraphrases. This reflects in part the tremendous change constantly taking place in the English language. Another important reason is the ongoing discovery of older and better manuscripts of both the Old and New Testament. The careful study of these has resulted in a better understanding of the original languages of the Scriptures and the total context of the Biblical world. Witness the impact of the many important archaeological finds during the last 50 years. The discerning incorporation of the principles of linguistics will also be a continuing factor as new translations make their appearance in the future.

A good translation of the Scriptures should faithfully reflect the original, be it Hebrew or Greek, and its proper nuance of meaning in its context in good English. This means that the translation should convey to the reader the same information which the original conveyed to its readers in such a way that the message is not changed in terms of either information lost or gained. This is much easier said than done, since both Hebrew and Greek are quite unlike the English. Without taking the term too literally, this may be defined as the *formal equivalence* approach in the broad sense.

The term *dynamic equivalence* has sometimes been used to express the ideal for a translator to achieve. Simply stated, this means that the meaning of the original is translated in such a way that presumably it means the same to the reader of today as it did to the reader of the original in his day. In practice it often results in changing the form of the original text in seeking to express an ancient idea or situation in terms of a present, current idiom. The result of this is often at the cost of faithful accuracy. Perhaps the best illustration of this is *The Good News Bible*.

Some translations in their quest to be as immediately intelligible to the reader as possible have been termed a "paraphrase." Strictly speaking, a paraphrase may mean a freely rendered restatement or rephrasing of a passage in a presumably clearer form in the same language without changing its meaning. The King James Version translates a Greek phrase in Colossians 3:12 as "bowels of mercies." A proper paraphrase for this term would be "compassion." However, what is normally meant by "paraphrase" is when a translator takes unwarranted liberties throughout in adding to, altering, and omitting the meaning of the original so that the equivalence of its meaning in the English is not properly transferred. A good example of this is *The Living Bible*.

The following are key considerations in selecting a translation or translations for use: 1. What is the underlying text? A good translation should be based on the best original texts available. 2. How accurate is the translation? As stated above, a translation should be as faithful to the original as possible and only as free as necessary to reflect its meaning. 3. What is the quality of the English? The language should be dignified and reverent but clear to the reader.

There is no single perfect translation, despite claims to the contrary. It is wise to select several translations. Some translations are not suitable for use in the church service. This is especially true of a paraphrase or of those which overstress dynamic equivalence in its broader form.

D. Selected Bibliography of Versions

The Complete Bible: An American Translation. Trans. J. M. Powis Smith, Edgar J. Goodspeed, *et al.* Chicago: University of Chicago Press, 1939.
> The Old Testament is based on the Massoretic Text, compared with other texts; the New Testament is based on the Westcott-Hort text. Includes the Apocrypha.

The Good News Bible. (GNB) Prepared by R. Robert Bratcher. New York: American Bible Society, 1976.
> Also known as *Today's English Version* (TEV). Dynamic equivalence in very broad form.

The Jerusalem Bible. (JB) Gen. ed. Alexander Jones. New York: Doubleday, 1968.
> Translated from the Hebrew and Greek, incorporating a study of the latest manuscript finds. The notes are a translation of the abridged French edition and at times reflect both Roman Catholic dogma and a critical approach. The translation is in contemporary idiom.

The New Jerusalem Bible. Gen. ed. Henry Wansbrough. New York: Doubleday, 1985.
> A comprehensive update of *The Jerusalem Bible* including revised notes.

King James Version (KJV) or *Authorized Version* (AV). Various Publishers.
> First published in 1611, this translation was based on late manuscripts. Some editions have revised some of its more archaic language. Despite the late manuscripts underlying it and its less modern language, for many it is still the standard against which other translations are judged.

The Holy Bible: An American Translation. Trans. W. F. Beck. New Haven, MO: Leader Publishing Co., 1976.
> The New Testament has been revised and is ready for printing. The Old Testament is undergoing revision.

The Living Bible, Paraphrased. (LB) Wheaton, IL: Tyndale, 1971.
> A loose paraphrase, heavily based on the American Standard

Version of 1901. It often departs from the meaning of the original.

The Modern Language Bible. Ed. Gerrit Verkuyl. Grand Rapids, MI: Zondervan, 1969.

A revised edition of the Berkeley Version in contemporary English.

New American Bible. (NAB) New York: P. J. Kennedy and Sons, 1970.

The first American Roman Catholic Bible translated from the original languages. It reflects a distinct Roman Catholic emphasis.

New American Standard Bible. (NASB) Various publishers.

A project of the Lockman Foundation, La Habra, CA, began as a revision of the American Standard Version. For the Old Testament the third edition of the Kittel Hebrew text together with readings from the Qumran texts were used, and the 23rd edition of the Nestle Greek Testament for the New Testament with modification in the direction of the "Received Text." Its English tends to be more stilted and less idiomatic.

New English Bible. (NEB) Oxford and Cambridge University Presses, 1970.

A joint project of the Protestant churches in England, the NEB translates rather freely, often more a paraphrase. It uses British expressions. In the New Testament an eclectic approach to variant readings is evident.

New International Version. (NIV) Grand Rapids, MI: Zondervan, 1978.

Sponsored by the New York International Bible Society, the NIV is the product of a joint project of evangelical scholars. The translators were concerned to reflect the best witness of the Hebrew text and versions. The eclectic approach to New Testament readings was followed. The translation approach is that of dynamic equivalence.

New King James Version. (NKJV) Nashville: Nelson, 1982.

An attempt to update the language while retaining the quality of the original KJV. For the Old Testament the readings found in most manuscripts were followed. The New Testament heavily reflects the late texts of the *Textus Receptus.*

New Testament in Modern English. J. B. Phillips. Rev. ed. New York: Macmillan, 1973.

A dynamic equivalence translation in a very broad sense, this paraphrase reads as if it were written in the 20th century. The revision is based on the United Bible Society's Greek text of 1966.

Revised Standard Version. (RSV) Various publishers, revised, 1971. Copyrighted by the Division of Christian Education of the National Council of Churches, the work of revision was authorized in 1937. The complete Bible translation was published in 1952 with subsequent revision. Its purpose is to reflect the witness of the latest manuscripts and to express the meaning of the original in language suited for both private and public worship, and seeking to preserve the language quality of the King James Version. A slightly revised version has been prepared for use in the Roman Catholic Church.

E. Annotated and Study Bibles

Recent years have seen a proliferation of a wide range of annotated, reference, and study Bibles. Careful examination before purchasing such helps is essential. Advertising claims sometimes do not carefully reflect the actual contents of the product.

What features should a good annotated Bible have? Among its features should be purposeful cross-references; a simple, factual introduction to each book including its theme; selected alternate readings of a given verse; and a selected concordance which lists the most important Bible terms and some references to where these are found. Current and accurate charts, maps, and also hopefully good illustrations should be included.

A good study Bible should feature the above together with selected comments about the importance of a given passage or section, and a few selected articles on the original texts and a simple explanation of rules of textual selection. Also essential are articles highlighting the importance of archaeological finds, brief descriptions of the geography and climate of especially Palestine, and the like. An index to proper names of people and places is also helpful. Some include a selected topical index. A reference Bible, such as the *Thompson Chain Reference Bible* features a unique reference system with code numbers to a number of passages listed under given topics with cross-references to others.

In addition to checking the above features, it is crucial to ascertain the theological views of the scholar or scholars who have prepared it. Are these views in harmony with the Scriptural witness itself? What about such issues as the doctrine of inspiration, the virgin birth of our Lord, and the historicity of events recorded in Scripture? Are millennial overtones evident in the helps?

The following are selected titles with a variety of study helps:

Barker, Kenneth, gen. ed. *The New International Study Bible—New International Version*. Grand Rapids, MI: Zondervan, 1985.

Includes general articles as well as introductory articles to each book of the Bible, annotations, charts, maps, illustrations and indexes, done by evangelical scholars. Rather heavy millennial emphases throughout.

Bruce, F. F., gen. ed. *The International Bible Commentary with the NIV*. Rev. ed. Grand Rapids, MI: Zondervan, 1986.

Contains general articles together with introductory articles to each book in the Bible, written by evangelical scholars. These reflect a careful knowledge of varying views of Scripture. Comments sometimes take a somewhat freer view, e.g., the authorship of the Pentateuch and Isaiah, the priority of Mark, and the like. Includes helpful maps and illustrations together with selected bibliographies after each article.

Hoerber, Robert, gen. ed. *Concordia Self-Study Bible—New International Version*. St. Louis, Concordia, 1986.

General articles including one on the principal teachings of Scripture, introductory articles on each book of Scripture, annotations, charts, maps, illustrations, indexes.

Lindsell, Harold, ed. *Harper Study Bible*. New York: Harper & Row, 1964.

Follows the general pattern of a study Bible, done by evangelical scholars, with a concern to remain respectful of Scripture.

May, Herbert G., and Bruce M. Metzger, eds. *The New Oxford Annotated Bible*. New York: Oxford, 1973.

The 1971 revised text of the RSV with an introduction to both the Old and New Testament. Also brief introductory articles to each book, which often reflect a critical view; brief annotations including also textual comments.

The Open Bible. Nashville: Nelson, 1978.

Available with either the KJV or NASB texts. The work of a group of evangelical scholars. A Biblical Cyclopedic Index in front lists over 8000 names, events, and doctrines with Scripture passages and a brief explanation or definition. Christian Life Study Outlines are found at the beginning of the New Testament and are repeated in separate study lessons in footnote form.

Thompson, Frank C., ed. *The New Chain-Reference Bible.* Indianapolis: B. B. Kirkbride, various dates.

Available in the KJV, RSV, or NIV text, this unique study Bible features a chain of cross-references in the margins on a wide variety of topics. The complete chain references are found in the back in alphabetical order together with the number assigned to each topic.

F. Selected Bibliography on the History of Translations

Ackroyd, P. R., et al., eds. *The Cambridge History of the Bible.* 3 vols. Cambridge: Cambridge University Press, 1963–70.

The three volumes offer a careful investigation into the history of the Bible in Western Christianity. Each of the following three volumes takes up the history in a given period. Volumes available as a set or individually, also in paperback form.

Ackroyd, P. R., and C. F. Evans, eds. Vol. 1: *From the Beginnings to Jerome.* 1970.

Lampe, G. W. H., ed. Vol. 2: *The West From the Fathers to the Reformation.* 1969.

Greenslade, S. L., ed. Vol. 3: *The West From the Reformation to the Present.* 1963.

Beekman, J., and J. Callow. *Translating the Word of God.* Grand Rapids, MI: Zondervan, 1974.

Two Wycliffe Bible Translators discuss and illustrate basic principles of translation.

Bruce, F. F. *The Books and the Parchments.* 3rd ed. revised. Old Tappan, NJ: Revell, 1963.

————. *History of the English Bible in English.* 3rd ed. New York: Oxford, 1978.

Sketches the history from the beginning of the English translations to the present. He stresses the principles that lie behind each translation.

Carson, Donald A. *The King James Version Debate—A Plea for Realism.* Grand Rapids, MI: Baker, 1978.
The proper role of textual criticism and other principles in the ongoing task of translating the Bible.

Glassman, E. *The Translation Debate.* Downers Grove, IL: Inter-Varsity, 1981.
Nontechnical presentation of various theories of translation; much helpful information.

Hills, M. T., and E. J. Eisenhart. *A Ready Reference History of the English Bible.* New York: American Bible Society, 1979.
A brief, simple guide to Bible translation.

Kubo, Sakae, and Walter Specht. *So Many Versions? Twentieth-Century Versions of the Bible.* Grand Rapids, MI: Zondervan, 1975.
A careful analysis of translations and paraphrases of this century.

Lewis, Jack P. *The English Bible from KJV to NIV—A History and Evaluation.* Grand Rapids, MI: Baker, 1981.
A careful review of major translations, the principles behind each, and samples of how these were applied.

Nida, Eugene A. *The Book of a Thousand Tongues.* Rev. ed. New York: American Bible Society, 1972.
A catalog of every language and dialect into which the Bible has been translated together with a sample.

von Campenhausen, H. F. *The Formation of the Christian Bible.* Philadelphia: Fortress, 1977.
Traces how the canons of the Old and New Testament developed and their shaping of the Scriptures.

VI

English Concordances, Dictionaries, and Encyclopedias

A. Concordances

1. Brief Overview

Important for the development of Bible concordances is the activity of Stephen Langdon (d. 1228). He served as expository lecturer at the University of Paris. He divided the books of the Bible into chapter divisions in the Vulgate. In 1550 John Marbeck published the first concordance of the Bible in English, but at this time the chapters had not as yet been divided into verses. This came somewhat later.

The man who made "concordance" a household word was Alexander Cruden of Aberdeen, Scotland. In 1737 he published *A Complete Concordance to the Holy Scriptures of the Old and New Testament*. As he himself acknowledged, it was not complete in the absolute sense. He made two revisions before his death in 1770.

In 1862 a Scotch bookseller, Robert Young, published his *Analytical Concordance to the Bible*. He went beyond Cruden and listed the Bible passages under each word. He included the Hebrew and Greek words underlying each English word. This assists the reader to analyze the different shades of meaning a word conveys. He transliterated the Greek and Hebrew letters to help readers to sound them out. He gave a brief definition of each word. He also listed some words with various shades of meaning in different categories—for example, he listed 15 categories of "son" together with the passages using the term in each category.

James Strong in 1890 issued *The Exhaustive Concordance of the Bible,* in which he listed every word in the King James Version. He included a special listing of every word in which either the KJV differed from the Revised Version or vice versa. He also added a dictionary of the Hebrew and "Chaldee" and the Greek words translated in the KJV together with their meaning and proper pronunciation.

In 1894 J. B. R. Walker issued *The Comprehensive Concordance to the Holy Scriptures.* Although quite similar to the work by Cruden, it is much more complete and has been a favorite of many Bible students.

In the same year, Orville James Nave published a topical or thematic Bible of the KJV. He developed a system of topics ranging from theology to archaeology, geography, life and customs, ancient religions and a host of other topics and listed pertinent passages under each of these. Although this resource needs revision, the soundness of its approach has been well demonstrated.

In time, as other translations were made, concordances of some of these major translations were prepared and published. The copyright of some of the older concordances has expired long ago. Such concordances are published in various degrees of completeness by a variety of publishers. Some have undergone revision and additions in study features.

2. The Use of a Concordance

Samuel Johnson described a concordance as "a book which shows in how many texts of Scripture any word occurs." Aside from seeking to find the location of a given passage, the proper use of a concordance can result in a very enriching experience.

The careful use of a concordance is of prime importance. Among others, the proper use of a concordance serves the following purposes: 1. to find the true meaning of a word in Biblical usage; 2. to determine the fine, distinctive shades of meaning of synonyms that have the same meaning in general; 3. to trace nuances of important grammatical constructions; 4. to study distinctive truths of any specific book or all of Scripture; 5. to trace the growth of a concept or theological motif in Scripture; 6. to trace the history of a given person, event, or place and references to the same in Scripture.

3. Selected Bibliography

Some of the concordances listed below are published by various publishers in either complete and or somewhat abridged form. It is always wise to examine such a resource to make sure that it has all the essential features for purposeful Bible study.

Cruden, Alexander, ed. *Cruden's Unabridged Concordance*. Grand Rapids, MI: Baker, 1979.

Darton, M. ed. *Modern Concordance to the New Testament*. Garden City, NY: Doubleday, 1977.

Based on the Greek text, this resource can be used with any of the major contemporary translations. Arrangement is both topical and by word. The Greek word underlying derivatives is included together with citations.

Elder, F. ed. *Concordance to the New English Bible: New Testament*. Grand Rapids, MI: Zondervan, 1964.

Ellison, John W., ed. *Nelson's Complete Concordance of the Revised Standard Version Bible*. 2nd ed. Nashville: Nelson, 1978.

Does not always give the Hebrew or Greek of the English word that has been translated. Words that occur most frequently in the Scriptures are omitted.

Goodrick, Edward W., and John R. Kohlenberger III, eds. *The NIV Complete Concordance*. Grand Rapids, MI: Zondervan, 1981.

Includes helpful cross-references to related verb forms. Not included are the origins of Hebrew and Greek words. Text printed in small typeface.

Hartdegen, S. J., ed. *Nelson's Complete Concordance of the New American Bible*. Collegeville, MN: Liturgical Press, 1977.

The concordance of the Roman Catholic translation, *The New American Bible* (NAB) of 1970.

Joy, C. R., ed. *Harper's Topical Concordance*. Rev. ed. New York: Harper & Row, 1976. Paperback.

Quotations are taken from the KJV.

Morrison, Clinton, ed. *An Analytical Concordance to the Revised*

Standard Version of the New Testament. Philadelphia: Westminster, 1979.

Follows the general pattern of Robert Young's *Analytical Concordance*. Designed for one who does not know Greek. The Greek word in Greek script and in transliteration is given for every English entry. It indicates when several Greek words are translated by a single English word. Where the RSV omits a Greek word or supplies a word not in the Greek, this is indicated. Features an index-lexicon in the back, listing the ways in which a Greek word is translated in the RSV.

Nave, Orville J., ed. *Nave's Topical Bible.* Nashville: Nelson, 1979.

Strong, James, ed. *The Exhaustive Concordance of the Bible.* Rev. ed. Nashville: Abingdon, 1980.

Thomas, Robert L., ed. *New American Standard Exhaustive Concordance of the Bible.* Nashville: Holman, 1981.

Follows the pattern of Strong's *Exhaustive Concordance* in very readable type. The headings and passages are from the NASB. Includes a Hebrew-Aramaic and also a Greek dictionary keyed to Strong's word order.

Young, Robert, ed. *Analytical Concordance to the Bible.* Rev. ed. Nashville: Nelson, 1980.

Based on the W. B. Stevenson revision in 1922. Contains more analytical features than Strong's.

B. Bible Dictionaries and Encyclopedias

1. Brief Overview

The first Bible dictionary of a sort was written by Eusebius, the bishop of Caesarea (d. ca. 340). For various reasons he compiled the *Onomasticon,* a resource on Palestine. In this work he provided information on about 600 places in Palestine that would be of interest to Christians and especially to pilgrims. He gave the geographical location of each site and the pertinent Biblical passages, together with other interesting comments.

The first dictionary in keeping with the meaning of the word was a two-volume work produced in 1722 by Augustin Calmet, a French Benedictine monk. Two supplementary volumes were added in 1728. This was reissued in several translations and editions. Perhaps the most frequently reprinted edition in English was that by Edward Robinson in one volume in 1832.

In 1820 J. G. B. Winer issued his two-volume *Biblisches Realwoerterbuch,* which was a distinct break from the Calmet tradition. The third revised edition appeared in 1847–48. Original in conception, this comprehensive volume remained a standard work in Germany for several generations. In 1937 Kurt Galling published his *Biblisches Reallexikon* (Tuebingen: J. B. Mohr [Paul Siebeck]). This was perhaps the best of other books in this field published in Germany.

Meanwhile in England John Kitto also broke from the Calmet pattern in his *A Cyclopaedia of Biblical Literature* (Edinburgh, 1843–45, two volumes; the third edition edited by W. L. Alexander in three volumes [Philadelphia, 1866]). Kitto developed a new pattern with stress on the New Testament, its literature, theology, and archaeology.

In the meantime John McClintock and James Strong edited their monumental *Cyclopaedia of Biblical, Theological, and Ecclesiastical Literature* in 10 volumes (New York: Harper & Brothers, 1867–81), followed by a two-volume supplement in 1887. The editors drew on articles in the resources by Kitto and Winer. This set has been a very useful encyclopedia with emphasis on historical matters.

Kitto's work was superseded by Sir William Smith's three-volume *Dictionary of the Bible* (London, 1860–63). A second edition edited by Smith and J. M. Fuller appeared in 1893. Assisted by 53 American and British scholars, Smith produced a vast storehouse of diverse knowledge: antiquities, biography, geography, and the natural history of the Old and New Testament and the Apocrypha in a comprehensive and thorough manner. Several abridged versions were published for popular use.

In 1898–1902 James Hastings together with J. A. Selbie, A. D. Davidson, S. R. Driver, and H. B. Swete published a four-volume work, *A Dictionary of the Bible* (New York: Scribners). An additional volume appeared in 1904 to update the set with regard to recent discoveries. The full title describes the wide range of the contents "dealing with the Bible's language, literature and contents, including the Biblical theology."

In 1909 James Hastings together with others edited a one-volume

Dictionary of the Bible, which claimed in the main to be a new and independent work, and not merely an abridgment of the larger work.

As a complement to the four-volume set, Hastings and J. A. Selbie edited *A Dictionary of Christ and the Gospels* (New York: Scribners, 1906–08). In this set they tried to give an account of everything that relates to Christ, His person, life, work and teachings. This set was followed by a lesser work *Dictionary of the Apostolic Church* (New York: Scribners, 1916–19).

Another major work appeared in 1915, edited by James Orr under the title *The International Standard Bible Encyclopaedia* (Chicago: The Howard Severance Co.) and revised by Melvin Grove Kyle in 1929. This set embodied the best scholarship and included the latest information written in a less technical manner. Although complete in its definition of words and terms as a dictionary, it arranged and grouped its material in the manner of an encyclopedia. This set is currently being revised.

A number of single-volume Bible dictionaries were published at the turn of the century. Among them is *A Dictionary of the Bible* by John D. Davis (Philadelphia, 1898). This together with the following title has gone through a series of new editions and revisions. For many years Davis' work was a very popular resource. The second title is *A New Standard Bible Dictionary,* edited by M. W. Jacobus, E. C. Lane, and A. C. Zenos, which first appeared in 1909 and has gone through several editions.

2. Evaluation and Use

What is the difference between a Bible dictionary and a Bible encyclopedia? A look at the titles given above suggests that the distinction is easily blurred. Strictly speaking, a Bible dictionary is an alphabetical listing of words found in the Bible with definitions or explanations given. Such words include the names of peoples and places, religious and doctrinal terms, terms of life and customs and the like.

Technically an encyclopedia is a collection of articles embracing the whole range of topics related to the Bible, which go well beyond what, strictly speaking, is the normal province of a dictionary. In practice, the strict division between the two is often blurred, as a casual examination of the key titles listed above bears out.

Before purchasing a Bible dictionary or encyclopedia, it is important to focus clearly one's specific needs. Will a single-volume resource suffice, or would a multivolume set better fit these specific needs? How current is the volume or the set? Who is/are the editor(s) and what is their background and training? What is the general trend of the work with reference to Scripture and biblical criticism?

Other questions should also be asked, such as: Are the definitions clearly and simply stated? Does it give at least a variety of Bible references to a given term or site in order to give a quick overview? Is the material given restricted to Biblical references and information, or are other ancient sources (for example, information from the writings of Josephus) cited? How up-to-date is the material concerning the most recent information from archaeology, epigraphy and other sources? How about alternative terms for people, places, and religious concepts? How complete are the cross-references where these are germane? Are up-to-date maps, layouts, and plans included? What kind of pictures are included? Are they current? Are they well-printed? Are balanced and current bibliographies included? These and similar points of evaluation are important to follow in choosing a suitable resource.

3. Selected Bibliography—One-Volume Resources

Achtemeier, Paul J., gen. ed. *Harper's Bible Dictionary*. New York: Harper & Row, 1985.
> A complete revision of an earlier edition by other editors. Provides useful information from a somewhat critical perspective. Contains many pictures, maps, and sketches.

Alexander, Pat, ed. *Eerdman's Family Encyclopedia of the Bible*. Grand Rapids, MI: Eerdmans, 1978.
> The title describes its broad but simple coverage. Well-illustrated.

Bruce, F. F., ed. *Nelson's Bible Encyclopedia for the Family*. Nashville: Nelson, 1982.
> Popularly written for especially young readers. Highly illustrated.

Davis, J. D., ed. Davis' Dictionary of the Bible. 5th ed. Old Tappan, NJ: Revell, 1972.

A reprint of an old standard, even though its content needs to be updated.

Douglas, J. D., ed. *The New Bible Dictionary.* 2nd ed. Wheaton, IL: Tyndale, 1982.

Perhaps the outstanding single Bible dictionary. Clear and up-to-date with the most recent information on archaeological, geographical, historical, and linguistic developments. Many articles provide bibliographies. Usually very respectful of Scripture.

Hastings, James, ed. *Dictionary of the Bible.* Rev. ed. New York: Scribners, 1963.

Revised by F. C. Grant and H. H. Rowley, this resource emphasizes history. Apocryphal materials receive good coverage. Some of its topics provide a dialog on conservative and critical views of Scripture.

Smith, William. *Smith's Bible Dictionary.* Rev. ed. Nashville: Nelson, 1979.

This revised edition reflects some updating from the original. Its informative articles are brief. Although old, this dictionary is still popular.

Tenney, Merrill, ed. *The Zondervan Pictorial Bible Dictionary.* Rev. ed. Grand Rapids, MI: Zondervan, 1969.

Tenney provides concise, reliable, and information-filled articles. Although highly illustrated, the illustrations are often not well done. Some articles include bibliographies.

Unger, Merrill F. *Unger's Bible Dictionary.* Chicago: Moody, 1966.

A revision of *Barnes' Bible Encyclopedia* to provide more current information on Bible sites and key theological concepts. Illustrated with pictures and maps.

4. Selected Bibliography—Multi-Volume Resources

Bromiley, G. W., ed. *The International Standard Bible Encyclopedia.* Grand Rapids, MI: Eerdmans, Vol. 1 (A–D), 1979; Vol. 2 (E–J), 1982; Vol. 3 (K–P), 1986; Vol. 4 (Q–Z) in process.

A complete revision of the original to bring it up-to-date. Articles have been written by scholars who are critically aware of the theological position of contemporary scholars. Conservative in theological stance. Articles seek to be comprehensive with selective bibliographies. Illustrated, with maps.

Buttrick, G., and K. Crim, eds. *The Interpreter's Dictionary of the Bible*. 4 vols., with Supplementary Volume. Nashville: Abingdon, 1962, 1976.

Perhaps the most exhaustive Bible encyclopedia in recent years. Written in technical style and usually from a critical viewpoint. Bibliographies are usually extensive. Illustrated, with maps. Both Christian and Jewish writers. The supplementary volume brings the set up-to-date. An indispensable tool for the scholar.

Hillyer, N., ed. *The Illustrated Bible Encyclopedia*. 3 vols. Downers Grove, IL: InterVarsity, 1980.

The revised text of the *New Bible Dictionary* with many useful and well-conceived illustrations, pictures, and maps together with accompanying captions. Selective, helpful bibliographies. A very helpful resource for the scholar, pastor, teacher, and church library.

Pfeiffer, C. F., H. F. Vos, and J. Rea, eds. *Wycliffe Bible Encyclopedia*. 2 vols. Chicago: Moody, 1975.

Basically for the non-specialist, this set seeks to be concisely comprehensive. The illustrations are not of the best quality.

Tenney, M. C., ed. *The Zondervan Pictorial Encyclopedia*. 5 vols. Grand Rapids, MI: Zondervan, 1975.

Features concise articles with good content. Many illustrations. KJV, ASV, and RSV used.

C. Dictionaries and Encyclopedias on Theology, Church History, and Judaica

Although not strictly in the category of Bible dictionaries and encyclopedias, the following resources provide a wide range of helpful information. Unfortunately, some of the older standard resources are out of print.

Bauer, J. B., ed. *The Encyclopedia of Biblical Theology: The Complete Sacramentum Verbi*. New York: Crossroad, 1981.

An abridged reprint of a former three-volume work. Its articles are clearly written. The stress is on the development of terms and concepts in the course of dogmatic and ecclesiastical thought. Done from a Roman Catholic perspective.

Cross, F. L., and E. A. Livingstone, eds. *The Oxford Dictionary of the Christian Church*. 2nd ed., with corrections and some revisions. New York: Oxford University Press, 1983.

An invaluable one-volume resource of concise information on many aspects of church history, together with carefully selected bibliographies. Over 6000 entries.

Douglas, J. D., and E. E. Cairns, eds. *The New International Dictionary of the Christian Church.*. 2nd rev. ed. Grand Rapids, MI: Zondervan, 1978.

A helpful and reliable resource on church history by evangelical scholars. Sometimes described as the evangelical counterpart of *The Oxford Dictionary of the Christian Church*.

Dowley, T., ed. *Eerdman's Handbook to the History of Christianity*. Grand Rapids, MI: Eerdmans, 1977.

Designed for the general reader. Many illustrations.

Leon-Dufour, X., ed. *Dictionary of Biblical Theology*. Rev. ed. New York: Seabury, 1973.

Takes up theological themes and ideas. Comprehensive. Designed for the general reader. Sometimes has a Roman Catholic emphasis.

———. *Dictionary of the New Testament*. New York: Harper & Row, 1980.

Brief articles on important New Testament names and terms. Greek words are transliterated. Includes selected Bible references. Simply written.

McClintock, John, and James Strong, eds. *Cyclopaedia of Biblical, Theological, and Ecclesiastical Literature*. 12 vols. Grand Rapids, MI: Baker reprint, 1968.

Rahner, Karl, ed. *Encyclopedia of Theology: The Concise Sacramentum Mundi*. New York: Crossroad, 1975.

An abridgment of a larger work, covers a large theological spectrum from the post-Vatican II perspective.

Rahner, Karl, et al., eds. *Sacramentum Mundi: An Encyclopedia of Theology*. 6 vols. New York: Herder, 1968–70.

Articles contributed by over 600 experts on a wide variety of theological topics. A distinct post-Vatican II emphasis.

Roth, C., ed. *Encyclopedia Judaica*. 16 vols. New York: Macmillan, 1971–72.

The updated successor to *The Jewish Encyclopedia* (New York:

KTAV, 1901–06, 1964). Covers a wide range of helpful material important for both a study of Judaica and the New Testament.

VII

Commentaries

A. Various Types

A discerning collection of good commentaries is an essential part of the library of the serious Bible student. To add to it judiciously enables one to keep on growing in a careful and deeper knowledge and understanding of individual books of Scripture.

A wide variety of commentaries are on the market. Some emphasize a devotional approach. Others are concerned to stress the meaning of Scripture for daily life. Still others seek to look quickly at the setting and language of the text and to give expository comments on its practical message.

A true exegetical commentary seeks to do what the Greek word *exegeesetai* means, namely, to interpret carefully each word and/or phrase of the original in its total context—linguistic, historical, and theological—and seek to find its true meaning in keeping with the overall theme, structure, and setting of the book of Scripture being interpreted. Such a commentary should always hold top priority and be represented in the library of the serious Bible student, and especially that of the pastor and scholar.

B. Criteria

A key criterion of a good commentary is the thoroughness of its scholarship, giving evidence of an intimate and respectful knowledge of Scripture in its total linguistic, historical, and theological context.

What are the criteria for making a discerning choice of a commentary? What kind of questions should be asked in examining a commentary under consideration for purchase?

The following are important questions to be asked in evaluating a commentary:

1. Who is the author?
2. What are his qualifications for writing this resource?
3. Where does he stand theologically with reference to Scripture, and with reference to the varying critical approaches to Biblical interpretation?
4. What is the nature, content, and extent of the introductory articles?
5. What does he see to be the theme of the book to be interpreted?
6. How is this reflected in its structure and his interpretation?
7. How careful and detailed is his treatment of the original words and/or phrases as he draws on the nuances of their meaning, the grammar, and sentence structure?
8. Does he demonstrate an intimate knowledge of the history and life situation of the book and of the readers, e.g., Paul's letter to the Philippians?
9. How well is he acquainted with the results of valid historical investigation: archaeology, social setting, life and customs, and other facets of the life and setting of the book and of the readers? Does his work reflect current research on these matters?
10. How carefully does he draw on the cardinal doctrines of Scripture as these are reflected in the book?
11. Does he carefully understand the decisive importance of the unity of Scripture and the analogy of Scripture?
12. Does he write clearly and simply, or is the content sometimes obscured in complicated verbiage?
13. Does he carefully stress the "then and there" meaning before turning to its implications for the "here and now" of the text?
14. How purposefully extensive is the bibliography? Does it demonstrate a wide acquaintance with the best studies through the years?

C. Series Versus Single-Volume Commentaries

Periodically a new commentary series is launched with a salvo of attractive and high-powered advertising literature urging the recipient to purchase the first volume at a discount and then receive each volume as it comes off the press. Such promotional blandishment should be ignored. Except for the specialist who may need to have such a series in his library, it is usually unwise for both scholarly and financial reasons to purchase a series.

What about a single-volume commentary? It is important to remember that any such resource is by its very nature limited. However, a careful choice of such a single source or two is a worthwhile investment. A good single-volume commentary should have a variety of carefully researched and written general articles on an assortment of topics. The discerning editor of such a resource emphasizes the importance of giving concise and precise information on a given passage or pericope. The suggestions offered above should be asked in considering the purchase of such a resource.

D. Selected Single-Volume Commentaries

Black, M., and H. H. Rowley, eds. *Peake's Commentary on the Bible.* Nashville: Nelson, 1962.

Moderately critical, reflects the "biblical theology" movement. The strengths of this resource are especially some of the general articles in the New Testament section.

Brown, Raymond E., Joseph A. Fitzmyer, and Roland E. Murphy, eds. *The Jerome Biblical Commentary.* Englewood Cliffs, NJ: Prentice-Hall, 1969.

Written and edited by Roman Catholic scholars, it basically reflects a moderately critical view suited to Roman Catholicism. Some of its many general articles are outstanding. Includes the Apocrypha. Helpful cross-referencing.

Guthrie, Donald, J. A. Motyer, A. M. Stibbs, and D. J. Wiseman, eds. *The New Bible Commentary: Revised* 3rd ed. Grand Rapids, MI: Eerdmans, 1970.

Writers from a Reformed evangelical background. Straightforward exposition of the text. Respectful of inspired Scripture. Deals with difficult words and phrases. General articles helpful.

Harrison, E. F., and Charles F. Pfeiffer. *The Wycliffe Bible Commentary.* Chicago: Moody, 1962.

Written by evangelical scholars, respectful of Scripture. Most passages are not commented on in depth.

Roehrs, Walter, and Martin Franzmann. *Concordia Self-Study Commentary.* St. Louis: Concordia, 1979.

More of an annotated Bible than a commentary. The introductory articles and comments in the Old Testament section are especially helpful—scholarly, succinct, and to the point.

E. Selected Commentary Series

Recent years have seen the publication of the first few volumes of several new series. Where appropriate, such volumes will be listed under specific books of Scripture. The initials after each title listed below serve as the abbreviation for that series.

Albright, W. F., and David Noel Freedman, eds. *The Anchor Bible.* (AB) Garden City, NY: Doubleday, 1964–.

In Old Testament, philologically up-to-date, and perhaps more useful than the New Testament volumes. Most in the latter category are theologically weak and brief. All reflect varying degrees of critical approaches.

Barclay, William. *The Daily Study Bible.* (BARCLAY) 2nd ed. Philadelphia: Westminster, 1975–76.

Basically critical and brief in character. The emphasis is usually on the life-situation in the first century A.D. Used with discerning judgment, this aspect of the series can be very helpful.

Bruce, F. F., ed. *The New International Commentary on the New Testament.* (NICNT) Grand Rapids, MI: Eerdmans, 1960–.

Exposition of units of thought rather than verse-by-verse. Stress on the meaning of the text, with technical nuances of Greek vocabulary, grammar, and syntax often in the footnotes. In most cases the introductory articles are carefully written. Generally conservative. Eighteen volumes projected. Some of the older volumes are being updated.

Buttrick, George A., ed. *The Interpreter's Bible Commentary.* (IB) 12 vols. Nashville: Abingdon, 1951–57.

Features the KJV and RSV in parallel columns at the top of each page with very brief exegesis and often extensive expository comments. Reflects varying critical approaches. The general articles in volumes 1 and 7 are in the main helpful; other volumes of little value compared to other available resources.

Clements, Roland E., and Matthew Black, eds. *New Century Bible Commentary.* (NCB) Grand Rapids, MI: Eerdmans, 1970–.

Still in process, the volumes issued so far reflect varying approaches from conservative to more critical, depending on the author. Often very helpful if used with discernment. Now published in a very well-bound special paperback format. Technical material in the footnotes.

Cross, Frank Moore, and Helmut Koester, general chairmen of eds. *Hermeneia—A Biblical and Historical Commentary on the Bible*. (HERMENEIA) Philadelphia: Fortress, 1971–.

Most of the volumes thus far published are translations from the German. These reflect Continental critical thought. The language often unusually heavy. The format and design of the books cause needless difficulty. Use of these commentaries requires ongoing careful discernment; hence, this series is for the advanced student only.

Driver, Samuel R., Alfred Plummer, and Charles A. Briggs, eds. *The International Critical Commentary*. (ICC) Philadelphia: Fortress (for T. & T. Clark, Edinburgh).

Begun late in the 19th century by a combination of American and British scholars, this series covering most of the Old and the New Testament is presently being updated in some instances and completed under the general editorship of J. A. Emerton and C. E. B. Cranfield. Through the years this series has been valued for its scholarship with special reference to philology and, in many instances, very helpful exegetical information. The volumes reflect varying critical approaches. Perhaps the volumes on the New Testament are more useful than those dealing with the Old Testament.

Gaebelein, F. F., ed. *The Expositor's Bible Commentary*. (EBC) 12 vols. Grand Rapids, MI: Zondervan, 1979–81.

This series stresses an overall exposition of the text. The NIV text is used. Volume 1 features a variety of helpful general articles. Each book commented on contains additional articles, an outline of the book, together with a basic bibliography. The series is the work of evangelical and occasionally somewhat neoevangelical scholars. Presently only Volume 6 (Isaiah, Jeremiah, Lamentations, Ezekiel; 1986) of the Old Testament has appeared. The New Testament volumes are complete.

Harrison, R. K., ed. *The New International Commentary on the Old Testament*. (NICOT) Grand Rapids, MI: Eerdmans.

Titles in this new series have begun to be published. So far these have been generally conservative with some neoevangelical overtones. More technical information usually in footnotes.

Hubbard, David A., and Glenn W. Barker, eds. *The Word Biblical Commentary.* (WORD) Waco, TX: Word, 1982–.

Thus far only several of the 52 projected volumes have appeared—20 of these will be on the New Testament. Authors listed vary from conservative to rather critical in their views on Scripture. This series follows a unique format. Extensive bibliographies.

Keil, C. F., and Franz Delitzsch. *A Biblical Commentary on the Old Testament.* (KD) 10 vols. Grand Rapids, MI: Eerdmans, 1971 reprint.

A standard Old Testament commentary by two outstanding conservative scholars. A careful study of the original text and its implications for Biblical theology. Although somewhat old, it is still a most helpful resource.

Lange, John Peter. *A Commentary on the Holy Scriptures.* Rev. ed. 12 vols. Grand Rapids, MI: Zondervan, 1980 reprint.

A series written by an outstanding German conservative scholar of the late 19th century, translated and revised by Philip Schaff.

Lenski, R. C. H. *An Interpretation of the New Testament.* 12 vols. Minneapolis: Augsburg, 1931–38.

Careful analysis of the Greek text, also in the light of the analogy of Scripture. Reflects amillennial scholarship. Concerned about the meaning for today in the light of the "then and there" meaning of the text.

Tasker, R. V. G., ed. *The Tyndale New Testament Commentaries.* (TNTC) 20 vols. Grand Rapids, MI: Eerdmans, 1957–. Paperback. Generally conservative with some neoevangelical overtones at times. Provides a careful overview of each book. Some especially rich in content. Selected titles presently being revised under the editorship of Leon Morris.

Wiseman, Donald J., ed. *The Tyndale Old Testament Commentaries.* (TOTC) Downers Grove, IL: InterVarsity, 1979–.

Fifteen volumes projected. Compact series by evangelical scholars. Comments brief but meaty, occasionally with a somewhat critical approach.

Wright, G. Ernest, John Bright, James Barr, and Peter Ackroyd, eds.

The Old Testament Library. (OTL) Philadelphia: Westminster. Presently around 25 volumes in this series have appeared. The series reflects the "Biblical theology" movement and varying critical approaches, depending on the individual writer. The series includes not only comments on Old Testament books but also studies on related topics.

F. Selected Commentaries on Individual Books of the Old Testament

1. Genesis

Aalders, G. S. *Genesis.* 2 vols. Grand Rapids, MI: Zondervan, 1981.
Good textual analysis. Addresses critical objections.

Allis, Oswald T. *The Five Books of Moses.* Philadelphia: Presbyterian and Reformed, 1949.
A chapter-by-chapter commentary on the Pentateuch with emphasis on the Mosaic authorship and its implications.

Cassuto, Umberto. *A Commentary on the Book of Genesis.* 2 vols. Jerusalem: Magnes Press, 1961–64. Vol. 1: *From Adam to Noah;* Vol. 2: *Noah to Abraham.*
Stresses Mosaic authorship. Filled with helpful comments.

Delitzsch, Franz. *A New Commentary on Genesis.* (KD) 2 vols. Edinburgh: T. & T. Clark, 1899.
A careful handling of theological issues in Genesis. Makes purposeful use of both Hebrew and Aramaic. A valuable resource.

Kidner, Derek. *Genesis. An Introduction and a Commentary.* (TOTC) Downers Grove, IL: InterVarsity, 1967.
A somewhat popular commentary by an evangelical scholar.

Leupold, Herbert C. *Exposition of Genesis.* 2 vols. Grand Rapids, MI: Baker, 1942.
A careful exposition by a conservative scholar.

Luther, Martin. *Lectures on Genesis.* Luther's Works—American Edition. 8 vols. Gen. eds. Jaroslav Pelikan and Helmut T. Lehmann. Various translators. St. Louis: Concordia, 1958–70.
Rather lengthy comments but patient, discerning reading of these volumes is rewarding.

Speiser, Ephraim A. *Genesis.* (AB) New York: Doubleday, 1964.

Although critical, Speiser provides information on the Near Eastern setting. Theologically rather thin.

Stigers, Harold G. *A Commentary on Genesis*. Grand Rapids, MI: Zondervan, 1976.

A very conservative resource.

von Rad, Gerhard. *Genesis*. (OTL) Rev. ed. Philadelphia: Westminster, 1973.

A very popular title in critical circles. Often supplements the form critical work of Hermann Gunkel. Must be used with careful discernment.

Westermann, Claus. *Genesis: A Commentary*. 3 vols. Tr. John J. Scullins. Minneapolis: Augsburg, 1984–86. (Vol. 1, Gen. 1–11; Vol. 2, Gen. 12–36; Vol. 3, Gen. 37–50.)

A highly technical work, summarizes the state of research with much comparative material, excursus, and linguistic notes. Minimal theology. Standard critical approach.

2. Exodus

Childs, Brevard S. *The Book of Exodus*. (OTL) Philadelphia: Westminster, 1974.

A useful, moderately critical resource. Carefully traces the history of interpretation and reacts against the more critical handling of the text. A "biblical theology" product.

Cole, Robert A. *Exodus*. (TOTC) Downers Grove, IL: InterVarsity, 1972.

A popular but generally helpful treatment of the text.

Davis, John D. *Moses and the Gods of Egypt: Studies in Exodus*. 2nd ed. Grand Rapids, MI: Baker, 1986.

A study of the text with special reference to the first 12 chapters in the light of recent archaeological and historical studies, with special reference to Egyptian religious and political customs.

Keil, C. F. *Biblical Commentary on the Pentateuch*. (KD) 3 vols. Grand Rapids, MI: Eerdmans, 1975 reprint.

3. Leviticus

Bonar, Andrew A. *A Commentary on the Book of Leviticus*. 4th ed. London: Banner of Truth, 1966.

A classic resource; homiletical tendencies.

Gray, George B. *Sacrifice in the Old Testament: Its Theory and Practice.* New York: KTAV, 1971.

Although critical, this is an important study on the role of sacrifice in the worship of Israel.

DeVaux, Roland. *Ancient Israel: Religious Institutions.* 2nd ed. Garden City, NY: Doubleday, 1968.

Mildly critical. One of the best available resources on Israel's worship.

Harrison, Roland K. *Leviticus: An Introduction and Commentary.* (TOTC) Downers Grove, IL: InterVarsity, 1980.

Generally evangelical; not theologically profound.

Noordtzij, A. *Leviticus: The Bible Student's Commentary.* Grand Rapids, MI: Zondervan, 1982.

Helpful exegetical insights; somewhat popular.

Wenham, Gordon. J. *The Book of Leviticus.* (NICOT) Grand Rapids, MI: Eerdmans, 1979.

A most helpful resource.

4. Numbers

Noordtzij, A. *Numbers.* Grand Rapids: Zondervan, 1983.

A sequel to the volume on Leviticus.

Wenham, Gordon J. *Numbers: An Introduction and Commentary.* (TOTC) Downers Grove, IL: InterVarsity, 1981.

Brief, somewhat popular; a good supplement to and update of the Keil-Delitzsch title.

5. Deuteronomy

Craigie, Peter C. *The Book of Deuteronomy.* (NICOT) Grand Rapids, MI: Eerdmans, 1976.

A careful, lucid exposition of the Biblical text.

Ridderbos, J. *Bible Student's Commentary: Deuteronomy.* Grand Rapids, MI: Zondervan, 1984.

Thompson, John A. *Deuteronomy: An Introduction and Commentary.* (TOTC) Grand Rapids, MI: Zondervan, 1974.

Generally very helpful resource.

6. Joshua

Boling, Robert G., and G. E. Wright. *Joshua.* (AB) New York: Doubleday, 1982.
Linguistically helpful but critical in viewpoint.

Davis, John J. *Conquest and Crisis: Studies in Joshua, Judges & Ruth.* Grand Rapids, MI: Baker, 1969.
A helpful resource by a conservative scholar.

Keil, C. F., and Franz Delitzsch. *Biblical Commentary on Joshua, Judges and Ruth.* (KD) Grand Rapids, MI: Eerdmans, 1971 reprint.

Woustra, Martin H. *The Book of Joshua.* (NICOT) Grand Rapids, MI: Eerdmans, 1981.
A helpful exposition; restrained typological emphasis.

7. Judges

Boling, Robert B. *Judges.* (AB) New York: Doubleday, 1975.
Philologically excellent; critical emphasis; most up-to-date.

Cundall, Arthur E., and Leon Morris. *Judges and Ruth.* (TOTC) Downers Grove, IL: InterVarsity, 1968.
Cundall uses a somewhat critical approach in his comments on Judges. Morris reflects recent archaeological information in his exposition of Ruth.

Wood, Leon. *The Distressing Days of the Judges.* Grand Rapids, MI: Zondervan, 1975.
A brief but fact-filled resource.

8. Ruth

Campbell, Edward F., Jr. *Ruth.* (AB) New York: Doubleday, 1975.
Strong on philology; generally helpful.

Morris, Leon. See above under Cundall.

9. 1 and 2 Samuel

Keil, C. F. *Biblical Commentary on the Books of Samuel.* (KD) Grand Rapids, MI: Eerdmans, 1971 reprint.

Although this title will not reflect more recent archaeological finds, it is still a helpful, standard resource.

McCarter, Peter K. *I Samuel*. (AB) New York: Doubleday, 1979.

————. *II Samuel*. (AB) New York: Doubleday, 1984.

Refers to the text-critical references in the Qumran literature in his expository comments. Critical.

Whybray, R. N. *The Succession Narrative: A Study of II Samuel 9–20, I Kings 1–2*. Studies in Biblical Theology, Second Series. Naperville, IL: Allenson, 1968.

10. 1 and 2 Kings

Gray, John. *I & II Kings: A Commentary*. (OTL) Philadelphia: Westminster, 1963.

Well-informed on Canaanite influences of the period. Critical. Strong on archaeology and comparative religions.

Jones, Gwilym H. *1–2 Kings*. (NCB) Grand Rapids, MI: Eerdmans, 1984.

Critical but sometimes helpful.

Keil, C. F. *Biblical Commentary on the Old Testament: The Books of the Kings*. (KD) Grand Rapids, MI: Eerdmans reprint.

Although somewhat old, it is a very helpful resource.

Montgomery, James A. *A Critical and Exegetical Commentary on the Books of Kings*. (ICC) Edinburgh: T. & T. Clark, 1951.

The historical data is handled well. Has been termed an outstanding example of text-critical scholarship.

Thiele, Edwin R. *The Mysterious Numbers of the Hebrew Kings*. 3rd ed. Grand Rapids, MI: Zondervan, 1984.

11. 1 and 2 Chronicles

Keil, C. F. *Biblical Commentary on the Old Testament: The Book of the Chronicles*. (KD) Grand Rapids, MI: Eerdmans reprint.

Myers, Jacob M. *I and II Chronicles*. (AB) New York: Doubleday, 1965.

Although he endorses JEDP, Myers holds to a single author of these two books. Also contends that Israel's worship and covenant guidelines were revealed by God. Stresses recent archaeological finds.

12. Ezra and Nehemiah

Clines, David J. R. *Ezra, Nehemiah, Esther.* (NCB) Grand Rapids, MI: Eerdmans, 1984.

Fensham, F. Charles. *The Books of Ezra–Nehemiah.* (NICOT) Grand Rapids, MI: Eerdmans, 1982.

Keil, C. F. *Biblical Commentary on the Books of Ezra, Nehemiah, and Esther.* (KD) Grand Rapids, MI: Eerdmans reprint.

Kidner, Derek. *Ezra–Nehemiah.* (TOTC) Downers Grove, IL: InterVarsity, 1979.
A helpful resource; somewhat popular.

Myers, Jacob M. *Ezra, Nehemiah.* (AB) New York: Doubleday, 1965.
Very helpful on the archaeological-historical data.

13. Esther

See 12. Ezra and Nehemiah.

Baldwin, Joyce. *Esther: An Introduction and Commentary.* (TOTC) Downers Grove, IL: InterVarsity, 1984.
Very helpful resource.

Moore, Carey A. *Esther.* (AB) New York: Doubleday, 1971.
Philologically the most up-to-date; theologically anemic.

14. Job

Andersen, Francis I. *Job: An Introduction and Commentary.* (TOTC) Downers Grove, IL: InterVarsity, 1976.
A very helpful resource considering the scope of the TOTC series.

Archer, Gleason, L. *The Book of Job.* Grand Rapids: Baker, 1982.
Popular, useful resource.

Delitzsch, Franz. *Biblical Commentary on the Book of Job.* (KD) 2 vols. Grand Rapids, MI: Eerdmans, reprint.
One of the great classic interpretations of Job.

Dhorme, Edouard. *A Commentary on the Book of Job.* London: Nelson, 1976.
A classic resource. Handles textual problems in detail.

Driver, Samuel L., and George B. Gray. *A Critical and Exegetical*

Commentary on the Book of Job. (ICC) 2 vols. Edinburgh: T. & T. Clark, 1921.

Philologically a rich resource.

Gordis, Robert. *The Book of God and Man: A Study of Job.* Chicago: University of Chicago Press, 1965.

A Jewish classic.

———. *The Book of Job.* New York: Jewish Theological Seminary of America, 1978.

Includes text of Job in Hebrew, a new translation, word studies, and commentary.

Habel, Norman C. *The Book of Job.* (OTL) Philadelphia: Westminster, 1985.

Considers Job a unity. Mildly critical.

Hulme, William E. *Dialogue in Despair: Pastoral Commentary on the Book of Job.* Nashville: Abingdon, 1968.

Helpful for purpose expressed in title.

Pope, Marvin H. *Job.* (AB) Rev. ed. New York: Doubleday, 1973.

Philologically very helpful, also with reference to Ugaritic comparative materials.

Rowley, Harold H. *Job.* (NCB) Grand Rapids, MI: Eerdmans, 1970.

Generally helpful and discerning.

14. Psalms

Alden, Robert. *Psalms: Songs of Discipleship.* (Everyman's) 3 vols. Chicago: Moody, 1975.

Popular treatment and brief with much information.

Alexander, Joseph A. *The Psalms Translated and Explained.* Grand Rapids, MI: Baker, 1979.

An old classic expository study of the Psalms. Studies some of the difficult passages with discerning maturity.

Anderson, Arnold A. *Psalms.* (NCB) 2 vols. Grand Rapids: Eerdmans, 1972.

Offers a clear and careful survey of recent opinion of each psalm. Moderately critical.

Dahood, Mitchell. *Psalms.* (AB) 3 vols. New York: Doubleday, 1966–70.

For the advanced and the well-informed student with special

reference to the place of the Ugaritic in ancient literature as Dahood saw it.

Delitzsch, Franz. *Biblical Commentary on the Psalms.* (KD) 3 vols. Grand Rapids, MI: Eerdmans, reprint.

An old standard by a great scholar of an earlier generation.

Kidner, Derek. *Psalms.* (TOTC) 2 vols. Downers Grove, IL: Inter-Varsity, 1973–75.

Written in a simple expository style—a very helpful resource. Reflects anti-cultic presuppositions.

Kimchi, David. *The Commentary of Rabbi David Kimchi on Psalms CXX-CL.* Trans. and Glossary by Ernest W. Nicholson and Joshua Baker. Cambridge: Cambridge University Press, 1973.

A Jewish exposition of psalms by a great Jewish scholar of the 12th century.

Kirkpatrick, Alexander F. *The Book of Psalms.* Grand Rapids, MI: Baker, 1982.

A reprint in the Thornapple Series. A helpful resource, reflecting some of the early British critical views.

Kraus, Hans Joachim. *Theology of the Psalms.* Tr. Keith Crim. Minneapolis: Augsburg, 1986.

Mildly critical. Helpful.

Leupold, Herbert C. *Exposition of the Psalms.* Grand Rapids, MI: Baker, 1959.

Reprint of a rich resource by a careful scholar. Often includes homiletical suggestions.

Luther, Martin. *First Lectures on the Psalms.* Luther's Works—American Edition. Vols. 10–11. Gen. eds. Jaroslav Pelikan and Helmut T. Lehmann. Trans. Herbert J. A. Bouman. St. Louis: Concordia, 1974, 1976.

———. *Selected Psalms.* Luther's Works—American Edition. Vols. 12–14. Gen. eds. Jaroslav Pelikan and Helmut T. Lehmann. Various translators. St. Louis: Concordia, 1955–58.

Special emphasis on the significance of the psalms from the vantage point of Good Friday and Easter.

Perowne, John J. S. *The Book of Psalms.* 2 vols. Grand Rapids, MI: Zondervan, 1976.

A reprint of an old conservative classic.

Weiser, Artur. *The Psalms.* (OTL) Philadelphia: Westminster, 1962.

Throughout points to the unifying covenant theme. Suffers at times from Weiser's hypothesis of a covenant festival.

14. Proverbs

Bridges, Charles. *An Exposition of the Book of Proverbs.* London: Banner of Truth, 1979.
   A reprint of a classic resource. Bridges shows how Proverbs with its practical truths relates to the rest of Scripture.

Delitzsch, Franz. *Biblical Commentary on the Proverbs of Solomon.* (KD) Grand Rapids, MI: Eerdmans, 1975 reprint.
   His exposition of Proverbs shows Delitzsch at his best as he carefully underlines the significance of the Hebrew text.

Kidner, Derek. *The Proverbs: An Introduction and Commentary.* (TOTC) Downers Grove, IL: InterVarsity, 1975.
   A master of the wisdom literature, Kidner packs much information in his comments.

————. *The Wisdom of Proverbs, Job and Ecclesiastes.* Downers Grove, IL: InterVarsity, 1985.
   Surveys the themes of Biblical wisdom as reflected in these books. He interacts with contemporary thought on wisdom literature and compares Old Testament with apocryphal wisdom literature and other parallels in ancient Near Eastern thought.

Scott, R. B. Y. *Proverbs.* (AB) New York: Doubleday, 1965.
   Draws parallels between Proverbs and pagan literature as he sees them. Exposition stresses the ethical content. Sometimes rather anemic.

17. Ecclesiastes

Delitzsch, Franz. *Biblical Commentary on the Song of Songs and Ecclesiastes.* (KD) Grand Rapids, MI: Eerdmans reprint.
   Both a philologically and theologically significant resource.

Eaton, M. *Ecclesiastes: Introduction and Commentary.* (TOTC) Downers Grove, IL: InterVarsity, 1983.
   Helpful in a popular format.

Ginsburg, Christian D. *The Song of Songs and Coheleth.* New York: KTAV, 1970 reprint.
   A major resource by a Jewish scholar who converted to Chris-

tianity. It is especially known for its histories of the interpretation of the books.

Gordis, Robert. *Koheleth: The Man and His World.* New York: Schocken, 1968 reprint.

Pays close attention to the Biblical idiom; includes rabbinical parallels. Sets Ecclesiastes in the traditions of the Persian and Hellenistic periods, rather than in that of Solomon.

Kidner, Derek. *The Message of Ecclesiastes.* (The Bible Speaks Today) Downers Grove, IL: InterVarsity, 1976.

———. *A Time to Mourn, and a Time to Dance: Ecclesiastes and the Way of the World.* Downers Grove, IL: InterVarsity, 1976. Somewhat popular but careful exposition.

Leupold, Herbert C. *An Exposition of Ecclesiastes.* Grand Rapids, MI: Baker, 1966.

A careful, discerning exposition of a difficult book.

Luther, Martin. *Ecclesiastes, Song of Solomon, and the Last Words of David (2 Samuel 23:1–7).* Luther's Works—American Edition. Vol. 15. Gen. eds. Jaroslav Pelikan and Helmut T. Lehmann. Various translators. St. Louis: Concordia, 1972.

Scott, R. B. Y. *Proverbs and Ecclesiastes.* (AB) New York: Doubleday, 1965.

Stresses recent literary and historical research; interpretation itself brief and critical in approach.

18. Song of Solomon

See titles listed above.

Carr, G. Lloyd. *The Song of Solomon: An Introduction and Commentary.* (TOTC) Downers Grove, IL: InterVarsity, 1984. Helpful in popular format.

Gordis, Robert. *The Song of Songs and Lamentations.* New York: KTAV, 1974.

Seeks to explore the importance of what he considers secular love songs being included in the Old Testament canon. Many rabbinical references.

Pope, Marvin H. *Song of Songs.* (AB) New York: Doubleday, 1977. Detailed philological study but strange views.

19. Isaiah

Alexander, Joseph A. *Commentary on the Prophecies of Isaiah.* Grand Rapids, MI: Zondervan, 1978 reprint.
A helpful old standard resource.

Delitzsch, Franz. *Biblical Commentary on the Prophecies of Isaiah.* (KD) 2 vols. Grand Rapids, MI: Eerdmans reprint.
An important classic resource.

Leupold, Herbert C. *An Exposition of Isaiah.* Grand Rapids, MI: Baker, 1977.
A careful exposition of Isaiah and its messianic prophecies.

Oswalt, John N. *The Book of Isaiah: Chapters 1–39.* (NICOT) Grand Rapids, MI: Eerdmans, 1986.
Stresses the theological and ideological unity as the primary datum; also that the essential content comes through Isaiah. A careful exegesis of the text.

Pieper, August. *Isaiah II: An Exposition of Isaiah 40–66.* Milwaukee: Northwestern, 1979.
Perhaps one of the best expositions of Isaiah 40–66.

Ridderbos, Jan. *Bible Student's Commentary: Isaiah.* Grand Rapids, MI: Zondervan, 1984.
Very helpful study.

Westermann, Claus. *Isaiah 40–66.* (OTL) Philadelphia: Westminster, 1969.
A moderately critical study.

Young, Edward J. *The Book of Isaiah.* (NICOT) 3 vols. Grand Rapids, MI: Eerdmans, 1965–72.
The *magnum opus* of a great conservative scholar. Carefully interprets the many prophecies of Isaiah in their context; also stresses their messianic import.

20. Special Studies on Isaiah

Allis, Oswald T. *The Unity of Isaiah.* Nutley, NJ: Presbyterian and Reformed, 1950.
Demonstrates the unity of the Book of Isaiah in a careful, discerning manner.

North, Christopher R. *The Suffering Servant in Deutero-Isaiah.* New York: Oxford, 1948.

Helpful; moderately critical.

Odendaal, Dirk H. *The Eschatological Expectation of Isaiah 40–66 with Special Reference to Israel and the Nations.* Nutley, NJ: Presbyterian and Reformed, 1970.

An important study.

Young, Edward J. *Studies in Isaiah.* Grand Rapids: Eerdmans, 1954.

Especially important for a careful study of Isaiah 7.

21. Jeremiah; Lamentations

Bright, John. *Jeremiah.* (AB) New York: Doubleday, 1965.

An important, mildly critical resource.

Gordis, Robert. *The Song of Songs and Lamentations.* New York: KTAV, 1974.

Harrison, Roland K. *Jeremiah and Lamentations: An Introduction and Commentary.* (TOTC) Downers Grove, IL: InterVarsity, 1973.

Emphasis on the historical data and its implications for Jeremiah's message. Somewhat popular.

Hillers, Delbert R. *Lamentations.* (AB) New York: Doubleday, 1972.

Some critical overtones, but helpful.

Keil, C. F. *Biblical Commentary on the Prophecies of Jeremiah.* (KD) 2 vols. Grand Rapids, MI: Eerdmans reprint.

Laetsch, Theodore. *A Bible Commentary: Jeremiah.* St. Louis: Concordia, 1952.

A helpful, careful exposition.

Orelli, Conrad von. *The Prophecies of Jeremiah.* Minneapolis: Klock & Klock, 1977.

A reprint of a pithy resource; mildly reflects critical views of the late 19th century.

Thompson, John A. *The Book of Jeremiah.* (NICOT) Grand Rapids, MI: Eerdmans, 1979.

Helpful, but linguistically and theologically rather weak.

22. Ezekiel

Eichrodt, Walter. *Ezekiel.* (OTL) Philadelphia: Westminster, 1970.

Perhaps the best of the "Biblical theology" movement. Only mildly critical.

Greenberg, Moshe. *Ezekiel I–XX.* (AB) New York: Doubleday, 1983. A helpful resource by a major Jewish scholar. Philologically strong.

Keil, C. F. *Biblical Commentary on the Book of Ezekiel.* (KD) 2 vols. Grand Rapids, MI: Eerdmans, reprint.

Levenson, Jon D. *Theology of the Restoration of Ezekiel 40–48.* Decatur, AL: Scholars Press, 1976.
A stimulating resource; sometimes critical.

Taylor, John B. *Ezekiel.* (TOTC) Downers Grove, IL: InterVarsity, 1969.
Helpful but somewhat critical.

Zimmerli, Walther. *Ezekiel..* (HERMENEIA) 2 vols. Philadelphia: Fortress, 1979, 1983.
Exhaustive; relatively critical, but helpful.

23. Daniel

Baldwin, Joyce. *Daniel: An Introduction and Commentary.* (TOTC) Downers Grove, IL: InterVarsity, 1978.
Very helpful resource.

Collins, John J. *Daniel. With an Introduction to Apocalyptic Literature.* Grand Rapids, MI: Eerdmans, 1984.
Critical, but helpful on the apocalyptic.

LaRondelle, Hans. *The Israel of God in Prophecy: Principles of Prophetic Interpretation.* Berrien Springs, MI: Andrews University Press, 1983.
A discerning study and refutation of dispensationalism.

Leupold, Herbert C. *An Exposition of Daniel.* Grand Rapids, MI: Baker, 1969.
A careful exposition of Daniel, emphasizing the Biblical basis for amillennialism.

Morris, Leon. *Apocalyptic.* Grand Rapids, MI: Eerdmans, 1972.
A very careful, well-informed introduction and treatment of the apocalyptic and its proper interpretation.

Porteous, Norman W. *Daniel.* (OTL) Philadelphia: Westminster, 1965.
A critical treatment with an attempt to deal with the theological significance of the Book of Daniel.

Rowley, Harold H. *Darius the Mede and the Four World Empires of*

Daniel. 2nd ed. Cardiff: University of Wales, 1959.

Russell, D. S. *The Method and Message of Jewish Apocalyptic: 200 B.C.–A.D. 100.* Philadelphia: Westminster, 1964.

A neoorthodox treatment of apocalyptic.

Whitcomb, John C. *Darius the Mede.* Philippsburg, NJ: Presbyterian and Reformed, 1959.

A standard resource from the conservative viewpoint.

Young, Edward J. *The Prophecy of Daniel: A Commentary.* Grand Rapids, MI: Eerdmans, 1949.

A careful exposition; amillennial.

24. Minor Prophets

Commentaries on the Twelve or combinations of several will be given in this listing.

Allen, Leslie C. *The Books of Joel, Obadiah, Jonah and Micah.* (NICOT) Grand Rapids, MI: Eerdmans, 1976.

Helpful. Jonah interpreted as a parable.

Baldwin, Joyce. *Haggai, Zechariah, Malachi: An Introduction and Commentary.* (TOTC) Downers Grove, IL: InterVarsity, 1972.

A helpful exposition; somewhat popular.

Feinberg, Charles L. *Minor Prophets.* Rev. ed. Chicago: Moody, 1976.

A good resource except for some millennial sections.

Hailey, Homer. *The Minor Prophets.* Grand Rapids, MI: Baker, 1972.

Includes a paraphrase of the text together with a brief exposition.

Keil, C. F. *Biblical Commentary on the Twelve Minor Prophets.* (KD) 2 vols. Grand Rapids, MI: Eerdmans, reprint.

Laetsch, Theodore. *Bible Commentary: The Minor Prophets.* St. Louis: Concordia, 1965.

A helpful resource by a careful scholar.

Pusey, Edward B. *The Minor Prophets.* 2 vols. Grand Rapids, MI: Baker, 1979.

A classic amillennial resource. Gives an overview of how selected churchmen throughout the years viewed the prophets.

Orelli, Conrad von. *The Twelve Minor Prophets.* Minneapolis: Klock & Klock, 1977 reprint.

A classic resource; moderately critical.

Wolff, Hans W. *Amos and Joel.* (HERMENEIA) Philadelphia: Fortress, 1977.

An important, exhaustive critical resource.

25. Hosea

Anderson, Francis I., and David Noel Freedman. *Hosea.* (AB) New York: Doubleday, 1980.

A very detailed resource, generally conservative.

Mays, James L. *Hosea.* (OTL) Philadelphia: Westminster, 1969.

Examines the theory of several strands of authorship; his thrust is on Hosea's message.

Ward, James M. *Hosea: A Theological Commentary.* New York: Harper & Row, 1966.

Stress on the text and its meaning.

Wolff, Hans W. *Hosea.* (HERMENEIA) Philadelphia: Fortress, 1974.

An exhaustive, critical work.

26. Joel

See "Minor Prophets" above.

27. Amos

Cripps, Richard S. *A Critical and Exegetical Commentary on the Book of Amos.* Rev. ed. Minneapolis: Klock & Klock, 1981.

An old standard; critical.

Mays, James L. *Amos.* (OTL) Philadelphia: Westminster, 1969.

Somewhat helpful; mildly critical.

28. Obadiah

See "Minor Prophets" above.

29. Jonah

See "Minor Prophets" above.

30. Micah

Hillers, Delbert. *Micah.* (HERMENEIA) Philadelphia: Fortress, 1984.
Moderately critical resource; thorough, helpful.
Mays, James L. *Micah.* (OTL) Philadelphia: Westminster, 1976.
Moderately critical; often helpful.

31. Nahum

Maier, Walter A. *Nahum.* (Thornapple) Grand Rapids, MI: Baker,
1980 reprint.
A detailed, thorough study.

32. Habakkuk, Zephaniah

See "Minor Prophets" above.

33. Haggai, Zechariah

Baldwin, Joyce. *Haggai, Zechariah, Malachi.* (TOTC) Downers
Grove, IL: InterVarsity, 1972.
Leupold, Herbert C. *An Exposition of Zechariah.* Grand Rapids, MI:
Baker, 1965.
A very helpful resource, careful in its interpretation of
apocalyptic.
Verhoef, Pieter A. *The Books of Haggai and Malachi.* (NICOT) Grand
Rapids, MI: Eerdmans, 1987.
A careful exposition of the text; sees each as a unity.

34. Malachi

Kaiser, Walter C., Jr. *Malachi: God's Unchanging Love.* Grand Rapids,
MI: Baker, 1984.
A very helpful resource, following a careful method of
interpretation.
Verhoef, Pieter A. *The Books of Haggai and Malachi.* (NICOT)
See above under Haggai.

G. Selected Commentaries on Individual Books of the New Testament

Note: See "E. Selected Commentary Series." Although not always mentioned under each book of the New Testament, most of the volumes in the Lenski and Tyndale series will prove helpful. Recent months have seen the beginning of releases of rather brief studies on the books of the New Testament. These need to be carefully checked to see if the contents measure up to the proper standard of good scholarship and contain at least enough adequate material to be useful.

1. Matthew

Carson, Donald A. *The Sermon on the Mount: An Evangelical Exposition of Matthew 5–7*. Grand Rapids, MI: Baker, 1978.
A masterful study of Matthew 5–7 in simple language, letting the text speak for itself.

————. *Matthew* in Volume Eight of *The Expositor's Bible Commentary*. (EBC) Grand Rapids, MI: Eerdmans, 1984.
A helpful resource with careful attention paid to pertinent aspects of Judaica. Favors Markan priority.

Davies, W. D. *The Setting of the Sermon on the Mount*. New York: Cambridge University Press, 1966.
A somewhat critical study. Davies' inclusion of helpful materials from Judaica, Qumran, and Pauline studies sheds light on the total context of this discourse.

Farmer, William R. *The Synoptic Problem: A Critical Analysis*. Rev. ed. Dillsboro, NC: Western North Carolina Press, 1976.
A careful study of the hypothetical priority of Mark, which shows that historically Matthew was the first gospel written.

Guelich, Robert A. *The Sermon on the Mount: A Foundation for Understanding*. Waco, TX: Word, 1982.
A vertical study, drawing in part on the hypothetical two-source hypothesis.

Hendriksen, William. *New Testament Commentary: Exposition of the Gospel According to Matthew*. Grand Rapids, MI: Baker, 1973.
This helpful resource keeps in mind the meaning of the text

then as well as its meaning for today. Technical materials often noted in the footnotes.

Hill, David. *The Gospel of Matthew.* (NCB) Grand Rapids, MI: Eerdmans reprint.

Moderately critical; brings in pertinent material from Judaica. Reflects Jeremias' work on the parables.

Lenski, R. C. H. *The Interpretation of St. Matthew's Gospel.* Minneapolis: Augsburg, 1943.

A standard resource concerned with being faithful to the text and with its implications for today.

Plummer, Alfred. *An Exegetical Commentary on the Gospel According to St. Matthew.* Grand Rapids, MI: Baker, 1982 reprint.

Although somewhat old, still a helpful resource by a well-known scholar of a previous generation. Follows to a degree the two-source hypothesis.

2. Mark

Anderson, Hugh. *The Gospel of Mark.* (NCB) Rev. ed. Grand Rapids, MI: Eerdmans, 1981.

Clear, up-to-date exposition.

Cole, Alan. *The Gospel According to St. Mark.* (TNTC) Grand Rapids, MI: Eerdmans, 1961.

Cranfield, C. E. B. *The Gospel According to Saint Mark: An Introduction and Commentary.* (CGTC) New York: Cambridge University Press, 1959.

Although somewhat critical, it is a helpful resource when used discerningly.

Hendriksen, William. *New Testament Commentary: Exposition of the Gospel According to Mark.* Grand Rapids, MI: Baker, 1975.

Lane, William. *The Gospel According to St. Mark.* (NICNT) Grand Rapids, MI: Eerdmans, 1973.

Perhaps the finest commentary on Mark. Pays close attention to the total context, also Judaica. Clearly and simply written.

Lenski, R. C. H. *Interpretation of St. Mark's Gospel.* Minneapolis: Augsburg, 1946.

Mann, C. S. *Mark: A New Translation with Introduction and Commentary.* (AB) Garden City, NY: Doubleday, 1986.

The general articles give a most helpful overview of the current scene of critical scholarship. Sees Mark as the third gospel account written which, together with Matthew and Luke, dates to the pre-A.D. 70 period. Stresses the great difficulty of the attempts to separate Jesus' actual words and deeds from what Jesus' followers later shared. Features very valuable extensive bibliographies and comments.

Martin, Ralph. *Mark: Evangelist and Theologian.* Contemporary Evangelical Perspectives. Grand Rapids, MI: Zondervan, 1973.
Provides a valuable overview.

Taylor, Vincent. *The Gospel According to St. Mark.* (Thornapple) 2nd ed. Grand Rapids, MI: Baker reprint.
A classic commentary, provides much detailed information on textual variants; somewhat neoorthodox in approach.

3. Luke

Ellis, E. Earle. *The Gospel of Luke.* (NCB) Rev. ed. Grand Rapids, MI: Eerdmans, 1983.
Helpful resource by a well-known evangelical scholar. Notes the two-source hypothesis in introduction.

Fitzmyer, Joseph A. *The Gospel According to Luke.* (AB) Garden City, NY: Doubleday, Vol. 1, 1981; Vol. 2, 1985.
Noted Semitic scholar; critical, with a careful understanding of the importance of Judaica. Use with discernment.

Hendriksen, William. *New Testament Commentary: Exposition of the Gospel According to Luke.* Grand Rapids, MI: Baker, 1978.
A helpful resource, mindful of the meaning also for today.

Lenski, R. C. H. *The Interpretation of St. Luke's Gospel.* Minneapolis: Augsburg, 1946.

Marshall, I. Howard. *The Gospel of Luke: A Commentary on the Greek Text.* (NIGTC) Grand Rapids, MI: Eerdmans, 1978.
Careful attention to original, presupposes the two-source hypothesis, arguing at times as to how much Luke borrowed from Mark; provides much helpful information on current, varying views on individual pericopes.

————. *Luke: Historian and Theologian.* Contemporary Evangelical Perspectives. Grand Rapids, MI: Zondervan, 1970.
A very valuable overview and evaluation of current studies and views.

Miller, Donald G. *Saint Luke.* (LBC) Atlanta: John Knox, 1959.
Somewhat brief; stresses prophecies of the Messiah and fulfillment, also in the light of Jewish messianic expectations.

Morris, Leon. *The Gospel According to St. Luke.* (TCNT) Grand Rapids, MI: Eerdmans, 1974.
An invaluable resource by a famous evangelical scholar.

Plummer, Alfred. *The Gospel According to St. Luke.*(ICC) 5th ed.
Edinburgh: T. & T. Clark, 1922.
A classic, valuable resource.

4. John

Barrett, C. K. *The Gospel According to Saint John.* 2nd ed. Philadelphia: Westminster, 1968.
Much information on current views on authorship and theology
of John; he himself holds to a version of the so-called "Johannine
School" hypothesis. Valuable for inclusion of pertinent information shed on the text by Judaica. Use with careful
discernment.

Brown, Raymond. *The Gospel According to St. John.* (AB) Garden
City, NY: Doubleday, Vol. 1, 2nd ed., 1979; Vol. 2, 1970.
Noted Roman Catholic scholar, holds to his own version of the
"Johannine School" hypothesis. Helpful if used discerningly.

Bruce, F. F. *The Gospel of John.* Grand Rapids, MI: Eerdmans, 1983.
A helpful resource by a famous scholar. Fails to note that John
uses Roman time references. This affects his interpretation of
several pericopes, including the passion narratives.

Carson, Donald A. *The Farewell Discourse and Final Prayer of Jesus:
An Exposition of John 14–17.* Grand Rapids, MI: Baker, 1980.
A topical, devotional exposition with emphasis on the theology
of the cross.

Hendriksen, William. *New Testament Commentary: Exposition of
the Gospel According to John.* Grand Rapids, MI: Baker, 1953.
A helpful resource in simple English.

Lenski, R. C. H. *The Interpretation of St. John's Gospel.* Minneapolis:
Augsburg, 1963.

Morris, Leon. *The Gospel According to St. John.* (NICNT) Grand
Rapids, MI: Eerdmans, 1970.
Perhaps the best commentary on John; demonstrates a wide and

careful knowledge of the total context.Written in a simple style with many valuable excurses.

——— . *Studies in the Fourth Gospel.* Grand Rapids, MI: Eerdmans, 1969.

A careful, scholarly study of the authorship, history, and theology of John and its relationship to the synoptics, in the light of current views in New Testament studies.

Plummer, Alfred. *The Gospel According to St. John.* Grand Rapids, MI: Baker reprint.

A helpful resource with brief, to the point comments.

Schnackenburg, Rudolf. *The Gospel According to St. John.* New York: Crossroad, Vol. 1, 1980; Vol. 2, 1981; Vol. 3, 1982.

Schnackenburg holds to his unique view of the "Johannine School" hypothesis. Volume 1 is a very helpful resource when used discerningly. Volume 2 is increasingly critical, and Volume 3 suffers heavily from the author's use of form and redaction criticism.

Westcott, B. F. *The Gospel According to St. John.* Grand Rapids, MI: Eerdmans, 1950 reprint.

An old standard; a helpful resource.

5. Acts

Bruce, F. F. *The Acts of the Apostles: The Greek Text with Introduction and Commentary.* 2nd ed. Grand Rapids, MI: Eerdmans, 1952.

A verse-by-verse exposition on the basis of the Greek text; helpful introductory articles.

Bruce, F. F. *The Book of Acts.* (NICNT) Grand Rapids, MI: Eerdmans, 1953.

Carefully explores each event recorded in the Book of Acts. A valuable resource.

Foakes Jackson, F. J., and Kirsopp Lake, eds. *The Beginnings of Christianity: Part I. The Acts of the Apostles.* 5 vols. Grand Rapids, MI: Baker, 1979 reprint.

Volumes 1 and 2 offer essays on Jewish, Gentile, and Christian backgrounds of the New Testament, and on the composition and authorship of Acts. Volume 3 is a dated study of the texts of Acts. Volume 4 is an exegetical exposition. Volume 5 contains very valuable articles on a wide variety of topics; it is the most valuable of the five volumes. Unfortunately available only in set form.

Harrison, Everett F. *Acts: The Expanding Church.* Chicago: Moody, 1976.

A very helpful exposition written in a simple style.

Hengel, Martin. *Acts and the History of Earliest Christianity.* Philadelphia: Fortress, 1979.

Hengel supports the historical integrity of Acts. In doing so, he interacts with the varying stances of critical scholars.

Longenecker, Richard N. *The Acts of the Apostles.* Vol. 9 of *The Expositor's Bible Commentary.* (EBC) Grand Rapids, MI: Zondervan, 1981.

Marshall, I. Howard. *The Acts of the Apostles.* (TCNT) Grand Rapids, MI: Eerdmans, 1980.

Presently the most up-to-date commentary on Acts by a careful scholar; contains some mildly critical overtones.

6. Romans

Barrett, C. K. *A Commentary on the Epistle to the Romans.* New York: Harper & Row, 1958.

A reasonably compact interpretation of Romans with stress on the theological and historical issues of this Pauline letter.

Bruce, F. F. *The Epistle of Paul to the Romans: An Introduction and Commentary.* (TCNT) Grand Rapids, MI: Eerdmans, 1963.

A helpful, succinct resource.

Cranfield, C. E. B. *A Critical and Exegetical Commentary on the Epistle to the Romans.* (ICC) Edinburgh: T. & T. Clark, Vol. 1, 1975; Vol. 2, 1979.

A valuable set of resources, perhaps more detailed than any other commentary. Use with discernment.

————. *Romans: A Shorter Commentary.* Grand Rapids, MI: Eerdmans, 1985.

A condensation of the two-volume set.

Franzmann, Martin H. *Romans: A Commentary.* St. Louis: Concordia, 1968.

A brief exposition of the text in its theological significance.

Kaesemann, Ernst. *Commentary on Romans.* Grand Rapids, MI: Eerdmans, 1980.

Stresses the theological meaning with emphasis on God's righteousness.

Lenski, R. C. H. *The Interpretation of St. Paul's Epistle to the Romans.* Minneapolis: Augsburg, 1936.

An old standard by a scholar concerned to reflect carefully the text and its meaning and significance for faith and life.

Luther, Martin. *Lectures on Romans.* Luther's Works—American Edition. Vol. 25. Gen. eds. Jaroslav Pelikan and Helmut T. Lehmann. Trans. Walter G. Tillmanns and Jacob A. O. Preus. St. Louis: Concordia, 1972.

Reflects Luther's notes used in his lecture series, during which he saw the full meaning of Romans 1:16–17.

7. 1 and 2 Corinthians

Barrett, C. K. *A Commentary on the First Epistle to the Corinthians.* New York: Harper & Row, 1968.

————. *A Commentary on the Second Epistle to the Corinthians.* New York: Harper & Row, 1974.

Both titles by Barrett are clear, comprehensive expositions, conscious also of the setting of the readers.

Bruce, F. F. *Commentary on First and Second Corinthians.* (NCB) Rev. ed. Grand Rapids, MI: Eerdmans, 1981.

A compact, clear exposition paying careful attention to the context of the readers in a masterful manner.

Harris, Murray J. *2 Corinthians,* Vol. 10 of *The Expositor's Bible Commentary* (EBC) Grand Rapids, MI: Zondervan, 1976.

Includes a study of the sequence of events leading to the writing of 2 Corinthians.

Lenski, R. C. H. *The Interpretation of St. Paul's First and Second Epistles to the Corinthians.* Minneapolis: Augsburg, 1963.

A valuable resource, much concerned to be faithful to the text and its setting as he expounds on the problems Paul faced in Corinth.

Morris, Leon. *The First Epistle of Paul to the Corinthians.* (TCNT) Grand Rapids, MI: Eerdmans, 1958.

Carefully expounds the message of 1 Corinthians in a simple manner.

Murphy-O'Conner, Jerome. *St. Paul's Corinth: Texts and Archaeol-*

ogy, Good News Studies 6. Wilmington, DE: Michael Glazier, 1983.

Excellent material on the total setting of Corinth, except for his comments on Gallio.

Plummer, Alfred. *A Critical and Exegetical Commentary on the Second Epistle of St. Paul to the Corinthians.* (ICC) Edinburgh: T. & T. Clark, 1915.

A rich, standard resource.

Robertson, A. T., and Alfred Plummer. *A Critical and Exegetical Commentary on the First Epistle of St. Paul to the Corinthians.* (ICC) 2nd ed. Edinburgh: T. & T. Clark, 1978.

A valuable, standard resource, paying attention also to classical parallels.

8. Galatians

Bruce, F. F. *The Epistle to the Galatians.* (NIGTC) Grand Rapids, MI: Eerdmans, 1982.

Very valuable, up-to-date commentary; shows the erroneous basis for the North Galatian hypothesis.

Burton, Ernest DeWitt. *A Critical and Exegetical Commentary on the Epistle to the Galatians.* (ICC) Edinburgh: T. & T. Clark, 1921.

A valuable resource, especially his extended comments on key words and issues.

Guthrie, Donald. *Galatians.* (NCB) Grand Rapids, MI: Eerdmans, 1973.

Lenski, R. C. H. *The Interpretation of St. Paul's Epistles to the Galatians, Ephesians, and Philippians.* Minneapolis: Augsburg, 1961.

A most helpful resource on Galatians, always keeping in mind the central issue of works versus grace. Not clear on the relationship between Galatians 2 and Acts 15.

Lightfoot, J. B. *St. Paul's Epistle to the Galatians.* New York: Macmillan, 1869, 1957 reprint.

Despite its age, still a helpful resource. Holds that Galatians was written during Paul's third missionary journey rather than, correctly, after his first journey.

Luther, Martin. *Commentary on St. Paul's Epistle to the Galatians.* Grand Rapids, MI: Baker, 1979 reprint.

Luther's comments on Galatians underline the crucial importance of justification by faith alone.

9. Ephesians

Abbott, T. K. *A Critical and Exegetical Commentary on the Epistles
to the Ephesians and to the Colossians.* (ICC) Edinburgh: T. &
T. Clark, 1897.
Heavy stress on philology, and valuable from that viewpoint.
Barth, Markus. *Ephesians.* (AB) 2 vols. Garden City, NY: Doubleday,
1974.
Very detailed study; use with careful theological discernment.
Bruce, F. F. *The Epistles to the Colossians, to Philemon, and to the
Ephesians.* (NICNT) Grand Rapids, MI: Eerdmans, 1984.
An excellent resource, carefully done.
Lenski, R. C. H. *The Interpretation of St. Paul's Epistles to the Ga-
latians, Ephesians, and Philippians.* Minneapolis: Augsburg,
1961.
Westcott, B. F. *Saint Paul's Epistle to the Ephesians.* Grand Rapids,
MI: Baker, 1979 reprint.
Still a helpful resource by a great New Testament scholar of the
past. Introductory articles include in parallel columns the re-
lationship of Ephesians to Colossians, other Pauline, and also
other apostolic writings. Helpful excurses appended.

10. Philippians

Bruce, F. F. *Philippians.* (GNC) New York: Harper & Row, 1953.
Holds to Pauline authorship. Brief, concise exposition. Needs
to be supplemented by a more detailed commentary.
Hawthorne, Gerald. *Philippians.* (WORD) Waco, TX: Word, 1983.
A careful, in-depth study. Opts for Caesarea as the place where
written.
Lenski, R. C. H. *The Interpretation of St. Paul's Epistles to the Ga-
latians, Ephesians and Philippians.* Minneapolis: Augsburg, 1961.
A standard resource by a scholar concerned with being faithful
to the text and the theology of the New Testament.
Lightfoot, J. B. *The Epistle of St. Paul to the Philippians.* Grand Rapids,
MI: Zondervan, 1953 reprint.

Careful exposition on the basis of the Greek text.

Martin, Ralph. *Carmen Christi: Philippians 2:5–11 in Recent Interpretation and in the Setting of Early Christian Worship.* Rev. ed. Grand Rapids, MI: Eerdmans, 1983.
Surveys the history and exegesis of these verses and their varied interpretations in Christological debates.

———. *Philippians.* (TCNT) Grand Rapids, MI: Eerdmans, 1960.
Provides insight into the text and its meaning; some attention to critical views.

———. *Philippians.* (NCB) Rev. ed. Grand Rapids, MI: Eerdmans, 1980.
An exposition conversant with a variety of critical theories. Use with careful discernment.

Vincent, Marvin R. *The Epistles to the Philippians and Philemon.* (ICC) Edinburgh, T. & T. Clark, 1897.
Helpful for the Greek and classical references.

11. Colossians and Philemon

Abbott, T. K. *The Epistles to the Ephesians and to the Colossians.* (ICC) Edinburgh: T. & T. Clark, 1897.
Helpful from the viewpoint of philology and the setting of the letters.

Bruce, F. F. *The Epistles to the Colossians, to Philemon, and to the Ephesians.* (NICNT) Grand Rapids, MI: Eerdmans, 1983.
An up-to-date, invaluable resource.

Lenski, R. C. H. *The Interpretation of St. Paul's Epistles to the Colossians, to the Thessalonians, to Timothy, to Titus and to Philemon.* Minneapolis: Augsburg, 1961.
A helpful resource by a careful student of the New Testament and its theology.

Lightfoot, J. B. *St. Paul's Epistles to the Colossians and to Philemon.* Grand Rapids, MI: Zondervan, 1957 reprint.
Still a helpful resource, includes the views of some of the early church fathers.

Martin, Ralph. *Colossians and Philemon.* (NCB) Rev. ed. Grand Rapids, MI: Eerdmans, 1981.
An important resource; includes an analysis of the nature of the

Colossian heresy, and a careful study of the provenance of these two letters.

Moule, C. F. D. *The Epistles of Paul to the Colossians and to Philemon.* (CGTC) New York: Cambridge, 1957.
Known for its careful study of the Greek text by a master exegete.

O'Brien, Peter T. *Colossians, Philemon.* (WORD) Waco, TX: Word, 1982.
Includes a full discussion of the pros and cons of debated matters, such as that of authorship, the setting of the letter, and the like.

12. 1 and 2 Thessalonians

Bruce, F. F. *1–2 Thessalonians.* (WORD) Waco, TX: Word, 1982.
Done in Bruce's usual thorough manner with careful attention to the meaning and implications of the Greek.

Frame, J. E. *A Critical and Exegetical Commentary on the Epistles of St. Paul to the Thessalonians.* (ICC) Edinburgh: T. & T. Clark, 1912.
An old standard, still a helpful resource.

Lenski, R. C. H. *The Interpretation of St. Paul's Epistles to the Colossians, to the Thessalonians, to Timothy, to Titus, and to Philemon.* Minneapolis: Augsburg, 1961.
A very helpful resource.

Marshall, I. Howard. *1 and 2 Thessalonians* (NCB) Grand Rapids, MI: Eerdmans, 1983.
A careful exposition, including introductory articles on the problems at Thessalonica, stressing the unity of 1 Thessalonians.

Morris, Leon. *The First and Second Epistles to the Thessalonians.* (NICNT) Grand Rapids, MI: Eerdmans, 1959.
———. *The Epistles of Paul to the Thessalonians.* (TCNT) 2nd ed. Grand Rapids, MI: Eerdmans, 1984.
Both titles give a careful, detailed exposition with attention to all the salient aspects of these two letters.

13. The Pastoral Epistles

Guthrie, Donald. *The Pastoral Epistles.* (TNTC) Grand Rapids, MI: Eerdmans, 1957.

A helpful resource with emphasis on the exposition of the text. Surveys the various suggestions as to authorship. Holds to Pauline authorship.

Kelly, J. N. D. *The Pastoral Epistles.* Grand Rapids, MI: Baker, 1981 reprint.

An excellent resource by the author of *Early Christian Creeds* and *Early Christian Doctrines.*

Lenski, R. C. H. *The Interpretation of St. Paul's Epistles to the Colossians, to the Thessalonians, to Timothy, to Titus and to Philemon.* Minneapolis: Augsburg, 1961.

Lock, Walter. *The Pastoral Epistles.* (ICC) Edinburgh: T. & T. Clark, 1924.

A rather concise, helpful resource. Uncertain on authorship.

Stott, John R. W. *The Message of 2 Timothy.* (The Bible Speaks Today). Grand Rapids, MI: Zondervan, 1973.

Originally published under the title "Guard the Gospel."

14. Hebrews

Bruce, F. F. *The Epistle to the Hebrews.* (NICNT) Grand Rapids, MI: Eerdmans, 1964.

A helpful resource, carefully expounds the many analogies drawing heavily on the Old Testament and their fulfillment in Christ (typology).

Guthrie, Donald. *The Epistle to the Hebrews: An Introduction and Commentary.* (TCNT) Grand Rapids, MI: Eerdmans, 1983.

Comments on the Christological emphases of Hebrews.

Hagner, Donald A. *Hebrews.* (GNC) New York: Harper & Row, 1983.

Divided into thematic sections; brief and to the point. Keeps in mind the Christological emphasis of Hebrews. Used best as a supplemental resource.

Hughes, Philip E. *A Commentary on the Epistle to the Hebrews.* Grand Rapids, MI: Eerdmans, 1977.

Heavy in theological emphasis and the role of Hebrews in church history; language rather complex.

Lenski, R. C. H. *The Interpretation of the Epistle to the Hebrews and the Epistle of James.* Minneapolis: Augsburg, 1966.

A lucid exposition with emphasis on the Christological emphases of the writer of Hebrews. Careful attention to typology.

Moffatt, James. *A Critical and Exegetical Commentary on the Epistle to the Hebrews.* (ICC) Edinburgh: T. & T. Clark, 1924.
Helpful because of its philological emphasis. Use with discernment.

Montefiore, Hugh. *The Epistle to the Hebrews.* New York: Harper & Row, 1964.
Holds that Hebrews was addressed to church at Corinth. Includes helpful introductory articles with stress on Apollos as the most probable author, with careful attention to typology. Use with discernment.

Westcott, B. F. *A Commentary on the Epistle to the Hebrews.* Grand Rapids, MI: Eerdmans, 1950 reprint.
Although somewhat old, still a helpful resource with special reference to the Greek and the early church fathers.

15. James

Davids, Peter. D. *The Epistle of James.* (NIGTC) Grand Rapids, MI: Eerdmans, 1982.
Sets this book in the social setting of Jewish Christians in the middle of the first century.

Kistemaker, Simon J. *Exposition of the Epistle of James and the Epistles of John.* Grand Rapids, MI: Baker, 1986.
Carefully prepared in the tradition of Hendriksen.

Laws, Sophie. *A Commentary on the Epistle of James.* New York: Harper & Row, 1980.
Favors Roman origin for letter, written by an anonymous writer who assumes the well-known name of "James." Use with discernment.

Lenski, R. C. H. *The Interpretation of the Epistle to the Hebrews and the Epistle of James.* Minneapolis: Augsburg, 1966.
Concerned to bring out the message of James with stress on the faith lived in life.

Mayor, J. B. *The Epistle of St. James.* 3rd ed. Grand Rapids, MI: Baker, 1978 reprint.
An old standard, very detailed and sometimes complex.

Ropes, J. H. *A Critical and Exegetical Commentary on the Epistle of St. James.* (ICC) Edinburgh: T. & T. Clark, 1978 reprint.
An old standard resource.

16. 1 and 2 Peter, Jude

Bigg, Charles. *A Critical and Exegetical Commentary on the Epistles of St. Peter and St. Jude.* (ICC) 2nd ed. Edinburgh: T. & T. Clark, 1902.

A very helpful resource with extensive introductory articles on the witness of the church fathers, authorship, and parallels with other New Testament writings. Bigg holds to the Petrine authorship of both letters, and stresses that Jude was written after 2 Peter.

Green, Michael. *The Second Epistle of Peter and the Epistle of Jude.* (TNTC) Grand Rapids, MI: Eerdmans, 1968.

A helpful resource. Holds to the Petrine authorship of 2 Peter. Suggests that a hypothetical document attacking false doctrines may antedate both epistles.

Kelly, J. N. D. *A Commentary on the Epistles of Peter and Jude.* Grand Rapids, MI: Baker, 1969.

Holds to the unity of 1 Peter and feels that the case for Petrine authorship is strong. In his view Jude was written prior to 2 Peter, with the latter written by an unknown author.

Lenski, R. C. H. *The Interpretation of the Epistles of St. Peter, St. John, and St. Jude.* Minneapolis: Augsburg, 1966.

Stibbs, Alan. M. *The First Epistle General of Peter.* (TNTC) Grand Rapids, MI: Eerdmans, 1959.

A very helpful resource. The introductory articles show an intimate knowledge of the variety of critical hypotheses. Holds to the Petrine authorship and the unity of 1 Peter.

17. The Johannine Epistles

Brooke, A. E. *A Critical and Exegetical Commentary on the Johannine Epistles.* (ICC) Edinburgh: T. & T. Clark, 1912.

A helpful resource. Holds that John's gospel and the Johannine letters were written by the same author, who may not have been the apostle. Introductory articles include valuable parallels between the epistles and the gospel.

Brown, Raymond E. *The Epistles of John.* (AB) Garden City, NY: Doubleday, 1982.

An exhaustive study which must be used with careful discernment.

Kistemaker, Simon J. *Exposition of the Epistle of James and the Epistles of John.* Grand Rapids, MI: Baker, 1986.

Introductory articles carefully analyze various theories on authorship, concluding that the apostle John is the author. Commentary in the fine tradition of Hendriksen.

Lenski, R. C. H. *The Interpretation of the Epistles of St. Peter, St. John, and St. Jude.* Minneapolis: Augsburg, 1966.

Marshall, I. Howard. *The Johannine Epistles.* (NICNT) Grand Rapids, MI: Eerdmans, 1978.

Holds that the three letters were written by the same person but is uncertain whether he can be definitely identified as the apostle John. Otherwise a helpful resource.

Stott, John R. W. *The Epistles of John.* (TNTC) Grand Rapids, MI: Eerdmans, 1964.

A careful exposition written in simple style. Carefully surveys various views on authorship and accepts the apostle John as author.

Westcott, B. F. *The Epistles of St. John.* 3rd ed. Grand Rapids, MI: Eerdmans, 1966 reprint.

A classic resource.

18. Revelation

Beasley-Murray, G. R. *The Book of Revelation.* Rev. ed. Grand Rapids, MI: Eerdmans, 1981.

Opts not to identify author; needs to be clearer on his understanding of Revelation 20. Otherwise helpful.

Becker, Siegbert W. *Revelation: The Distant Triumph Song.* Milwaukee: Northwestern, 1985.

A careful exposition, stresses that a millennial view is not in keeping with the text and message. The apostle John identified as author. Surveys and analyzes the validity of other suggestions as to authorship.

Caird, G. B. *The Revelation of St. John the Divine.* New York: Harper & Row, 1966.

Uncertain on authorship. Holds that until late, Jews did not believe in afterlife. Imprecise on his understanding of Revelation 20. Use with discernment.

Hendriksen, William. *More Than Conquerors: An Interpretation of the Book of Revelation.* Grand Rapids, MI: Baker, 1978 reprint.
A careful exposition of the text, keeping in mind the apocalyptic literary form and John's true message. A classic resource.

Lenski, R. C. H. *The Interpretation of St. John's Revelation.* Minneapolis: Augsburg, 1963.
A resource concerned with faithfully expounding the true message of Revelation.

Morris, Leon. *The Revelation of St. John.* (TNTC) Grand Rapids, MI: Eerdmans, 1969.
A helpful resource by a careful Johannine scholar.

Mounce, R. H. *The Book of Revelation.* (NICNT) Grand Rapids, MI: Eerdmans, 1977.
Tentatively suggests John the apostle as author. Holds to an earthly millennium as proper interpretation for Revelation 20. Use with discernment.

Sweet, J. P. M. *Revelation.* (Pelican) Philadelphia: Westminster, 1978.
Especially helpful for insight into Jewish apocalyptic thought as reflected in Revelation. Holds to an unknown author. More precise definitions of some terms would have been helpful. Use with discernment.

VIII

Hermeneutics

A. Its Meaning and Importance

The term "hermeneutics" designates both the science and the art of interpretation. Its essential purpose is to arrive at the exact meaning of Scripture.

Biblical hermeneutics can be defined as the technique of Biblical interpretation, following given steps and principles of interpretation growing out of and based on Scripture. Before seeking to arrive at the meaning of a given text for the present, it is essential, by following the proper principles and methods, to arrive at the meaning of the text for the original writer and his readers *then*.

B. Selected Bibliography

The following titles reflect some of the standard titles in hermeneutics together with a selection of recent studies, which seek to reflect a careful Biblical stance.

Allis, Oswald T. *Prophecy and The Church.* Philadelphia: Presbyterian and Reformed, 1945.
   A very careful study of premillennial dispensationalism and its lack of a Biblical basis.

Beckwith, Roger. *The Old Testament Canon of the New Testament Church.* Grand Rapids, MI: Eerdmans, 1985.

Berkhof, Louis. *Principles of Biblical Interpretation: Sacred Hermeneutics.* Grand Rapids, MI: Baker, 1950.

Davidson, Richard M. *Typology in Scripture: A Study of Hermeneutical Structures.* Berrien Springs, MI: Andrews University Press, 1981.

An excellent study of the New Testament use of the term *typos.*

Fee, Gordon D. *New Testament Exegesis: A Handbook for Students and Pastors.* Philadelphia: Westminster, 1983.

Goppelt, Leonhard. *Typos: The Typological Interpretation of the Old Testament in the New.* Grand Rapids, MI: Eerdmans, 1982.
A classic study of typology.

Girdlestone, Robert E. *Synonyms of the Old Testament: Their Bearing on Christian Doctrine.* 2nd ed. Grand Rapids, MI: Eerdmans reprint.

Goldingay, John. *Theological Diversity and the Authority of the Old Testament.* Grand Rapids, MI: Eerdmans, 1986.

Kaiser, Walter. *Toward an Exegetical Theology: Biblical Exegesis for Preaching and Teaching.* Grand Rapids, MI: Baker, 1981.
A collection of essays on major problems of interpretation.

———. *The Uses of the Old Testament in the New.* Chicago: Moody, 1985.
The author examines his topic from the apologetic, prophetic, typological, theological, and practical viewpoints.

Levinson, John D. *Sinai and Zion: An Entry into the Jewish Bible.* New York: Winston, 1985.
Stresses the unity of the covenant event at Mount Sinai and Zion in the Old Testament. Mildly critical.

Mickelsen, A. Berkeley. *Interpreting the Bible.* Grand Rapids, MI: Eerdmans, 1963.
A valuable resource, widely used as textbook.

Ramm, Bernard. *Hermeneutics.* Grand Rapids, MI: Baker, 1971.

———. *Protestant Biblical Interpretation: A Textbook on Hermeneutics.* Grand Rapids, MI: Baker, 1970.
Two valuable studies by a famous evangelical scholar.

Stuart, Douglas. *Old Testament Exegesis: A Primer for Students and Pastors.* Philadelphia: Westminster, 1980.

Terry, Milton S. *Biblical Hermeneutics: A Treatise on the Interpretation of the Old and New Testaments.* 2nd ed. Grand Rapids, MI: Zondervan reprint.
A classic resource.

Wright, Christopher J. H. *An Eye for An Eye: The Place of Old Testament Ethics for Today.* Downers Grove, IL: InterVarsity, 1983.
Examines the theological, social, and economic framework for

Old Testament ethics and explores a variety of Old Testament themes and their implications for life today.

Young, Edward J. *My Servants the Prophets*. Grand Rapids, MI: Eerdmans, 1952.
A valuable study of the prophet and his role.

C. Varying Critical Approaches

The last decades especially have seen the ongoing development of critical approaches to the interpretation of Scripture, approaches which through the years grew out of the Enlightenment. These more recent approaches to interpretation have at times been described as being neutral and part of the scientific approach.

However, a cursory reading of such critical material will indicate that these works approach the interpretation of Scripture with basic presuppositions. Among these is a view that does not recognize the uniqueness of Scripture as being in its totality the Word of God. Also basic to these approaches is the presumption of the gradual development of the Old Testament in varying strands of tradition until these developed into what we know now as the Old Testament.

Similar theories abound with reference especially to the gospels. The task of the interpreter is to determine what Jesus actually said and did and what was added in the process of transmission until each gospel was written. Implicit in such an approach is the view that, since human beings were involved in writing the gospels, these products also participate in misconceptions and human error.

D. Selected Bibliography

The amount of literature written by those who either use such an approach or have done a careful analysis of its validity is enormous. The following is a very selective list of some of the important titles which shed light on such approaches and their validity as these writers see it.

1. Guides to Biblical Scholarship.

The following titles, each in less than a hundred pages, seek to define and describe the nature, purpose, and function of the discipline indicated in the respective titles. Recent years have witnessed varying forms of development within these areas, depending on the individual practitioner of each discipline. Each of these guides is published by Fortress Press in Philadelphia.

Krentz, Edgar. *The Historical-Critical Method.* 1975.

Habel, Norman C. *Literary Criticism of the Old Testament.* 1971.

Tucker, Gene M. *Form Criticism of the Old Testament.* 1971.

Rast, Walter E. *Tradition History and the Old Testament.* 1972.

Miller, J. Maxwell. *The Old Testament and the Historian.* 1976.

Beardslee, William A. *Literary Criticism of the New Testament.* 1970.

Petersen, Norman R. *Literary Criticism for New Testament Critics.* 1978.

McKnight, Edgar V. *What is Form Criticism?* 1969.

Perrin, Norman. *What is Redaction Criticism?* 1973.

Patte, Daniel. *What is Structural Exegesis?* 1976.

Doty, William G. *Letters in Primitive Christianity.* 1979.

2. Selected Critical Resources.

Collins, Raymond F. *Introduction to the New Testament.* Garden City, NY: Doubleday, 1983.

Collins makes an integral use of the critical method in his treatment of the New Testament.

Grant, Robert, and David Tracy. *A Short History of the Interpretation of the Bible.* 2nd ed., rev. and enlarged. Philadelphia: Fortress, 1984.

Included in this short history is the rise of rationalism and its development into various critical approaches to the Scriptures, which both writers see as necessary for the interpretation of Scripture, however not in their extreme form.

Hayes, John H.. and Carl P. Holloday. *Biblical Exegesis: A Beginner's Handbook.* Atlanta: John Knox, 1982.

Stresses the use of the critical approach as essential for exegesis and shows how to use it.

Kuemmel, Werner Georg. *The New Testament: The History of the Investigation of Its Problems.* 2nd ed. Nashville: Abingdon, 1972.

After a brief survey of the ancient through the Reformation periods, Kuemmel carefully traces key men and factors in their interpretation of the New Testament, beginning with English Deism and progressing into the present era. Includes selections from the works of the men under consideration. This resource helps one more fully to understand the current state of the critical methodology.

Neill, Stephen. *The Interpretation of the New Testament, 1861–1961.* New York: Oxford, 1966.

A masterful survey of the topic, including the ongoing development and refinement of the critical approach and ends with the author's assessment at the time of writing.

Soulen, Richard N. *Handbook of Biblical Criticism.* 2nd ed. Atlanta: John Knox, 1981.

Provides succinct information of important names, titles, and approaches to Biblical criticism and interpretation. An extremely helpful resource.

Stuhlmacher, Peter. *Historical Criticism and Theological Interpretation of Scripture: Toward a Hermeneutics of Consent.* Philadelphia: Fortress, 1977.

Begins with stating the problem of historical criticism, sketches the interpretation of Scripture through the centuries up to the present, analyzes the current dilemma in interpretation, and suggests a way out, stressing a hermeneutics of consent.

3. Selected Bibliography of Analyses of the Critical Approach

Carson, Donald A., and John D. Woodbridge, eds. *Hermeneutics, Authority, and Canon.* Grand Rapids, MI: Zondervan, 1986.

Nine chapters, each written by an evangelical scholar, analyzing the effects of varying approaches to Scripture and its proper interpretation.

Hasel, Gerhard. *New Testament Theology: Basic Issues in the Current Debate.* Grand Rapids, MI: Eerdmans, 1978.

———. *Old Testament Theology: Basic Issues in the Current Debate.* 3rd ed., rev. and expanded. Grand Rapids, MI: Eerdmans, 1975.

Both titles make a careful analysis of problems in interpretation and the negative effect of the critical approach.

Ladd, George E. *The New Testament and Criticism.* Grand Rapids, MI: Eerdmans, 1967.

An analysis of the critical approach in New Testament interpretation by a well-known evangelical scholar.

Longenecker, Richard N., and Merrill C. Tenney, eds. *New Dimensions in New Testament Study.* Grand Rapids, MI: Zondervan, 1974.

A collection of essays by evangelical scholars on: I. canon, text and background; II. Jesus and the gospels; III. Paul and the epistles. These involve analysis of various aspects of the critical approach.

Maier, Gerhard. *The End of the Historical-Critical Method.* St. Louis: Concordia, 1977.

Marshall, I. Howard, ed. *New Testament Interpretation: Essays on Principles and Methods.* Grand Rapids, MI: Eerdmans, 1977.

These essays analyze the current scene of New Testament interpretation. Part I takes up the background; Part II, the use of critical methods; Part III, the task of exegesis; and Part IV, the New Testament and the modern reader. Essays III, VII–XI, and XV–XVI especially involve an analysis of the critical approach.

IX

Introductions and Bible History

A. Place and Purpose in Bible Study

The 66 books of the Bible were written over a long period of time and provide a vast amount of information on theology, history, culture, and geography. To gain a better understanding of the context in which each book of the Bible was written, it is wise to consult a book of isagogics or, as some prefer to say, of introduction.

A book of isagogics or introduction deals with questions that "introduce" a Biblical book, providing information on the author, the time when it was written, its intended audience and their circumstances, the purpose, and the history of the book within the canon of Scripture. In other words, a book of isagogics carefully takes up the who, what, when, where, to whom, and for what purpose of each book.

Such a volume necessarily deals with the theology of each book of Scripture: how it ties in with the unifying theme of God's covenant, and His specific message for those addressed in each of the individual books of Scripture.

Indeed, purposeful Bible study pays close attention to the theology of each book of Scripture. This fact presupposes that the book has a theological plan, purpose, and message, one which has meaning also for today. This involves basic hermeneutical presuppositions, themselves based on Scripture, namely, that the Scriptures are truly the inspired Word of God, that what they say is fact and without error. Where the respective author of an isagogical book stands in his theological approach to Scripture will become readily apparent. This is true also of other books dealing with Scripture.

B. Old Testament

1. Approaches to the Old Testament

Books on Old Testament isagogics usually fall into one of two categories. One approach deals with the Old Testament from the viewpoint of the total reliability of Scripture—that Moses, for example, is the true author of the Pentateuch. The second approach is critical. This normally involves some form of the documentary hypothesis and/or source analysis, which in one way or another questions the authorship of the books of the Old Testament and its trustworthiness as a book of history and theology.

2. Selected Bibliography

Armerding, Carl E. *The Old Testament and Criticism*. Grand Rapids, MI: Eerdmans, 1983.
    Discusses the various methodological approaches to the Old Testament, which are reflected in books on isagogics. He does so from the conviction that Scripture is the inspired Word of God.

Archer, Gleason L. *A Survey of Old Testament Introduction*. Rev. ed. Chicago: Moody, 1974.
    An evangelical scholar, Archer provides a careful study of the books of the Old Testament and also gives a discerning analysis of critical views on the various books of the Old Testament.

Childs, Brevard. *Introduction to the Old Testament as Scripture*. Philadelphia: Fortress, 1979.
    Childs introduces his book with introductory essays on the problem of the canon, canon and criticism, and text and canon. He then shows how Jews of the intertestamental period selected the writings which are found in the Old Testament and rejected other writings current in their time. He stresses that the 39 books of the Old Testament are not only a source of the Judeo-Christian tradition but also a product of that tradition.

————. *Old Testament Theology in a Canonical Context.* Philadelphia: Fortress, 1986.

The object of theological reflection and study is the books that form the Old Testament canon. The canonical approach views history from the perspective of Israel's faith as reflected in the Old Testament and seeks to follow the Biblical text in its theological use of history. Scripture serves as a continuing medium through which the saving events of Israel's history are appropriated by each new generation of faith.

Eissfeldt, Otto. The Old Testament: An Introduction. New York: Harper & Row, 1965.

This title together with those by Fohrer and Kaiser are the standard critical isagogical resources in wide use today. Each of these three writers has his own specific critical approach to the Old Testament.

Fohrer, Georg. *Introduction to the Old Testament* Nashville: Abingdon, 1970.

Harrison, Roland K. *Introduction to the Old Testament.* Grand Rapids, MI: Eerdmans, 1969.

An encyclopedic survey from an evangelical viewpoint. The writer includes a mass of information on the history of Old Testament interpretation, archaeology, chronology, textual criticism, Old Testament history, religion, and theology. This is followed by a book-by-book analysis of isagogical issues from both a critical perspective and a stance respectful of Scripture. Includes a section on the Apocrypha.

Hummel, Horace D. *The Word Becoming Flesh: An Introduction to the Origin, Purpose, and Meaning of the Old Testament.* St. Louis: Concordia, 1979.

Written from a careful Biblical viewpoint. The author examines the isagogical questions of the Old Testament and analyzes its interpretation and criticism. He highlights the theology of the Old Testament and its implications for the proper understanding of Scripture.

Kaiser, Otto. *Introduction to the Old Testament.* Oxford: Basil Blackwell, 1975.

Together with titles by Eissfeldt and Fohrer, presents a critical approach to the Old Testament.

Rendtorff, Rolf. *The Old Testament: An Introduction.* Tr. John Bowden. Philadelphia: Fortress, 1986.

A critical introduction in three parts: Part I takes up Israel's history and seeks to reconstruct historical development by introducing information from outside of the Bible. Part II looks at Old Testament literature as an expression of Israel's life, following the approach of Hermann Gunkel. Special emphasis is on the "life situation" and genres as the author sees them, as these reflect the family, clan, tribe, local community, legal matters, the cult, political institutions, and prophecy. Also discusses limitations of the form critical method. Part III takes up each book in its final form and discusses them in terms of various critical categories, e.g., the Deuteronomist stamp on the historical books.

Unger, Merrill F. *Introductory Guide to the Old Testament.* Grand Rapids, MI: Zondervan, 1951.

The author approaches his study from the conviction that the Scriptures are the Word of God and intimately part of history. He includes a careful analysis of critical hypotheses.

Young, Edward J. *An Introduction to the Old Testament.* Rev. ed. Grand Rapids, MI: Eerdmans, 1960.

A careful, incisive study of Old Testament isagogics by a great, well-informed evangelical scholar. Written in a winsome style.

C. New Testament

1. Approaches to the New Testament

Books on New Testament isagogics usually fall into one of three categories. One approach looks at the books of the New Testament in keeping with the witness of Scripture and that of the early church.

The second follows the critical approach with its emphasis on the hypothetical, decisive role of literary, form, and redaction criticism. This may also involve some form of what is termed structuralism as it is increasingly being practiced by some today. The critical approach sees the four gospels having their life situation in the post-A.D. 30 era and hence reflecting the life situation of the early church rather than that of Jesus. This approach usually includes the Hegelian dialectic, pitting a hypothetical Jewish Christianity against a hypothetical Hellenistic (Gentile) Christianity, and in time emerging out of this conflict comes catholic or universal Christianity. The critical approach usually also holds that some of the Pauline letters are pseudo-Pauline. Similar questions are also raised against some of the general epistles.

The third approach is a mediating one, seeking to be more respectful of Scripture and yet giving credence to some aspects of the critical approach, such as the non-historical Markan priority and the hypothetical Q. This is sometimes termed the neoevangelical approach. As is true of the critical, this approach is also found in several variations.

2. Selected Bibliography

The following selected bibliography includes some of the less technical books of isagogics which to some degree may emphasize more the present author's views of the content of the New Testament and its history. Unfortunately, several standard titles are presently out of print.

Barker, Glenn W., W. L. Lane, and J. R. Michaels. *The New Testament Speaks.* New York: Harper & Row, 1969.
    To set the stage for isagogical chapters, the initial chapters survey the canon and the historical setting of the New Testament. The authors seek to reflect the history and witness of Scripture. They do espouse the hypothetical Markan priority and hence date Matthew and Luke somewhere between 75–90. The date and place of writing for the captivity letters is left uncertain.

Franzmann, Martin H. *The Word of the Lord Grows: A First Historical Introduction to the New Testament.* St. Louis: Concordia, 1961.
    A careful study of the New Testament on the basis of its own witness and that of the early church with a helpful stress on the theological content of each of the books.

Guthrie, Donald. *New Testament Introduction.* 3rd ed. Downers Grove, IL: InterVarsity, 1971.
    A comprehensive, well-informed resource, by an author who seeks to be faithful to the Biblical witness. Somewhat uncertain on the interrelationships of the synoptic gospels—seems to favor

the hypothetical Markan priority and the existence of a "sayings" source. Presents a careful study and usually a discerning analysis of critical views.

Harrison, Everett F. *Introduction to the New Testament*. Grand Rapids, MI: Eerdmans, 1971.

A well-informed, basically conservative resource which carefully analyzes the various theories on authorship and possible origins. Tends toward the Markan priority with reference to the synoptics.

Kuemmel, Werner G. *Introduction to the New Testament*. Rev. ed. Nashville: Abingdon, 1975.

A complete revision and updating of the 17th edition of Feine-Behm in English translation, this is the standard resource of critical scholarship. This book gives evidence of the careful and wide acquaintance of the author with the issues in New Testament isagogics.

————. *The New Testament: The History of the Investigation of Its Problems*. 2nd ed. Nashville: Abingdon, 1972.

Although not an isagogical work, this resource presents a most helpful survey of the history of interpretation, beginning with the Reformation (though there is a very brief sketch of the ancient and medieval periods) and ending with the current era. Where appropriate, parts of the primary texts of various scholars of the past are included in English translation together with the setting and a discerning analysis.

Martin, Ralph P. *New Testament Foundations: A Guide for Christian Students*. Grand Rapids, MI: Eerdmans, Vol. 1, 1975; Vol. 2, 1978.

These two volumes survey the books of the New Testament in terms of the current issues of debate and interpretation. Both volumes contain much helpful information. Conclusions sometimes fall into the neoevangelical category.

Robinson, John A. T. *Redating the New Testament*. Philadelphia: Westminster, 1976.

The author's basic presupposition is that all books of the New Testament were written in Palestine before A.D. 70. This necessarily involves shaping the evidence to fit the conclusion. His rather radical conclusion and resultant suggestions have had an interesting effect on the world of New Testament scholarship and therefore merit inclusion in this listing.

D. Bible History

The following is a selection of the more standard titles in each of the two categories. There are a number of other titles, some of which may emphasize isagogical aspects more than history.

1. Selected Bibliography—Old Testament

Bright, John. *A History of Israel.* 3rd ed. Philadelphia: Westminster, 1981.

Bright provides a very knowledgeable history of the Old Testament era. He seeks to portray God's often unfaithful people in their total context. In this he is perhaps unsurpassed. He holds a critical perspective, but this title is one of the best Old Testament histories when used with careful discernment.

Harrison, Roland K. *Old Testament Times.* Grand Rapids, MI: Eerdmans, 1980.

Harrison draws on the history and cultures of Israel's surrounding nations in word and picture to provide a very helpful perspective for a better understanding of Old Testament history.

Pfeiffer, Charles F. *Old Testament History.* Grand Rapids, MI: Baker, 1973.

Draws on a wide variety of archaeological finds to provide a helpful history of Israel. Some of his chronology is somewhat later than Biblical chronology permits.

Schultz, Samuel J. *The Old Testament Speaks.* 3rd ed. New York: Harper & Row, 1980.

Demonstrates a careful acquaintance with the results of archaeological and epigraphical finds in the Near East which shed much light on the history of Israel. Written in an attractive, simple style.

Wood, Leon. *A Survey of Israel's History.* Rev. David O'Brien. Grand Rapids, MI: Zondervan, 1986.

A much used resource now updated. Includes a chapter on the intertestamental period.

2. Selected Bibliography—New Testament

Bruce, F. F. *New Testament History.* Garden City, NY: Doubleday, 1977.

Has been termed "the scholar's history of the New Testament" written in simple English. Presents a carefully researched, well-balanced historical account, seeking to be faithful to the witness of Scripture and history.

Filson, Floyd V. *A New Testament History: The Story of the Emerging Church.* Philadelphia: Westminster, 1964.

The author looks at the New Testament era in its larger context before taking up the life and ministry of Jesus and then that of Paul and the other writers. Holds to a late date for the gospels and the interpretative work of early church.

Goppelt, Leonhard. *Apostolic and Post-Apostolic Times.* Grand Rapids, MI: Eerdmans, 1977.

Stresses the internal development of the early church in the light also of varying views of New Testament scholarship.

Lohse, Eduard. *The New Testament Environment.* Nashville: Abingdon, 1976.

This title as well as that by Bo Reicke are standard introductions to the world of the New Testament.

Reicke, Bo. *The New Testament Era.* Philadelphia: Fortress, 1968.

Tenney, Merrill C. *New Testament Survey.* Rev. Walter M. Dunnett. Grand Rapids, MI: Eerdmans, 1985.

A widely used college text, this title provides an illustrated overview of the New Testament era and its 27 books in their historical context.

———. *New Testament Times.* Grand Rapids, MI: Eerdmans, 1965.

X

Biblical Theology

A. Theology of the Old Testament

Various approaches are taken in studying the theology of the Scriptures. These involve not only the methodological approach but also varying theological presuppositions, such as the writer's view of Scripture as either the inspired Word of God in its totality or a critical approach to Scripture.

A good summary of the history of Old Testament theology and a careful survey of the various hermeneutical and methodological approaches is provided by Gerhard Hasel in his *Old Testament Theology: Basic Issues in the Current Debate* (Grand Rapids, MI: Eerdmans, 3rd ed., 1982). Hasel begins with a history of interpretation and theology. Then he summarizes, analyzes, and points out problems in the various approaches and their basic presuppositions. He concludes with a selected yet rather comprehensive bibliography. His study centers especially on German theologians.

Because of the various approaches used by writers on the theology of the Old Testament, it is best to list selected titles under various categories.

1. The Dogmatic Approach

This approach usually follows the usual divisions used in systematic theology, namely, God-man-salvation or theology-anthropology-soteriology. The disadvantage of this approach is that it tends to impose thought patterns and categories which are foreign to the Old Testament. Many of the older works on theology used this approach.

A rather recent title along these lines which merits careful attention is:

119

Dyrness, W. *Themes in Old Testament Theology*. Downers Grove, IL: InterVarsity, 1979.

Dyrness seeks to reflect faithfully what the Scriptures say, and he does so on a somewhat popular level.

2. The Thematic Approach

This method seeks to use a theme or key concept as an organizing principle for the presentation of Old Testament theology. This procedure faces the problem that the wide diversity of thought in the Old Testament does not always lend itself to such an approach. This must always be kept in mind in using such a resource.

Eichrodt, Walter. *Theology of the Old Testament*. Philadelphia: Westminster, Vol. I, 1961; Vol. II, 1967.

This is a monumental work and follows through the covenant theme, or as it has been expressed: "the establishment of God's rule in this world."

Kaiser, Walter C. *Toward an Old Testament Theology*. Grand Rapids, MI: Zondervan, 1978.

A resource by an evangelical scholar, follows the thought of "divine blessing-promise," which includes but is broader than that of covenant.

Martens, Elmer A. *God's Design: A Focus on Old Testament Theology*. Grand Rapids, MI: Baker, 1981.

Martens stresses the theological significance of the land of Canaan in God's design for His people.

Themes include deliverance, community, knowledge of God, and the abundant life.

McCarthy, Dennis J. *Treaty and Covenant: A Study in Form in the Ancient Oriental Documents and in the Old Testament*. Analecta Biblica 21. Rome: Pontifical Institute, rev. 1978.

Looks at ancient treaty forms and parallels to covenant in the Old Testament. Follows critical presuppositions.

Vos, Gerhardus. *Biblical Theology*. Grand Rapids, MI: Eerdmans, 1948.

One of the earlier "Biblical theology" products, Vos' "theme" is "the revelation of God in history" as seen in the three "epochs" of Moses, the prophets, and the New Testament.

3. The "Diachronic" Approach

This approach assumes that there are various theologies in the Old Testament which were unfolded in the course of Israel's history, and therefore must be examined in their respective "layers." This procedure usually either employs evolutionistic presuppositions or results in evolutionistic conceptions. A monumental work in this category is:

von Rad, Gerhard. *Old Testament Theology*. New York: Harper & Row, Vol. 1, 1962; Vol. 2, 1965.

> von Rad insists that the Old Testament is a narration of "Heilsgeschichte," and therefore simply a "re-telling" of that. A major drawback is that such "re-telling" is ambiguous and subjective, and results in a lack of good Biblical theology.

4. The "New Biblical Theology" Approach

This approach is, in a sense, in opposition to the "diachronic" method and its "divorce" of the past and present. Brevard S. Childs is the champion of this approach. He insists that the whole Bible is the context of theology, that one cannot use noncanonical history and cultural contexts, and that there are no separate Old and New Testament theologies. A result is that the relationship between Old Testament theology and Biblical theology is uncertain.

Childs, Brevard S. *Introduction to the Old Testament as Scripture*. Philadelphia: Fortress, 1979.

> Childs claims that the "final canonical form" of Scripture is normative for theology, in contrast to those who maintain that formational and traditional processes are also valid contexts from which to formulate Biblical theology.

———. *Old Testament Theology in a Canonical Context*. Philadelphia: Fortress, 1986.

> In this recent title, the author stresses that the object of theological reflection and study is that of the Old Testament canon.

B. New Testament Theology

1. Overview

An informative resource on the history of New Testament theology and a careful survey of various approaches taken toward it is provided by Gerhard Hasel in his *New Testament Theology: Basic Issues in the Current Debate* (Grand Rapids, MI: Eerdmans, 1978). He traces the beginnings and development of New Testament theology from the Reformation period to the present. He sketches four varying approaches and their impact. He looks at the center and unity of New Testament theology and its relationship to the Old Testament. He concludes with six basic proposals toward a theology of the New Testament.

2. Selected Bibliography

The past decades have seen the appearance of a variety of resources with varying approaches to New Testament theology. The following are among the most important of such titles. Since in several instances these titles can be listed under various approaches, descriptive information will be given under each title rather than listing the volumes under suggested categories.

Bultmann, Rudolf. *Theology of the New Testament.* New York: Scribners, Vol. 1, 1951; Vol. 2, 1955.

Bultmann's approach to New Testament theology is deeply rooted in the "history of religions school," with a decisive emphasis on his specific use of historical criticism, dialectical theology, and existentialism. In his view the historical Jesus is obscured by the Christ of faith and the *kerygma* created by the early church, which made of Jesus the resurrected Christ. This must be demythologized to arrive at what he considered the true meaning for today.

Goppelt, Leonhard. *Theology of the New Testament.* Grand Rapids, MI: Eerdmans, Vol. 1, 1981; Vol. 2, 1983.

Limits his definition of salvation history to promise and fulfillment. Following his own critical approach, he holds that a core of manifestly authentic material gives a coherent picture of Jesus when it is extracted from the inauthentic material. Volume 2 presents Goppelt's view of the post-Pentecost "development" of the witness and understanding of Jesus as this is seen in each specific community situation. He explores the varying interpretations of the churches addressed in the epistles and those churches in which the final versions of Matthew, Mark, Luke, and John developed.

Guthrie, Donald. *New Testament Theology.* Downers Grove, IL: InterVarsity, 1981.

The author's *magnum opus,* reflecting a lifetime of study and research. Demonstrates the writer's extensive and intimate acquaintance with the total subject matter, following the order of systematic theology. Enhanced by carefully selected, pertinent footnotes and extensive bibliography. Features a very extensive section on Christology. Seeks always to be faithful to Scripture. A valuable resource.

Jeremias, Joachim. *New Testament Theology: The Proclamation of Jesus.* (Vol. 1 of his *New Testament Theology.*) New York: Scribners, 1971.

Through the use of his specific approach to form criticism, he seeks to strip away what he considers to be later additions in order to discover the very words and deeds of the "historical" Jesus. The final chapter seeks to relate the proclamation of Jesus to the resurrection in the earliest traditions and the interpretations of the church's witness.

Kuemmel, Werner Georg. *The Theology of the New Testament According to Its Major Witnesses: Jesus-Paul-John.* Nashville: Abingdon, 1973.

Kuemmel represents the "modern historical" approach. He attempts to set the preaching of Jesus, the theology of Paul, and the message of Christ in John's gospel against the background of the various primitive communities. His final chapter seeks to determine the unified central message of these key witnesses. A moderately critical reconstruction.

Ladd, George E. *A Theology of the New Testament.* Grand Rapids, MI: Eerdmans, 1974.

Stresses God's special revelation in history centered on what He has done in and through Jesus Christ as recorded in Scripture. This resource is divided into six parts: the synoptics, the fourth gospel, the primitive church (Acts), Paul, the general epistles, and the Apocalypse. The interpretation of Revelation reflects the author's specific views. Otherwise a very helpful resource.

Walther, C. F. W. *Law and Gospel.* Selected Writings of C. F. W. Walther. Gen. ed. August R. Suelflow. Trans. Herbert J. A. Bouman. St. Louis: Concordia, 1981.

Drawing on Scripture, the author demonstrates the crucial importance of making the proper distinction between Law and Gospel. An invaluable study.

XI

Theological Topics

Biblical theology by its very nature is very extensive and includes a wide variety of topics and subtopics. Space does not permit such a wide inclusion of topics with their selected bibliographies. Some topics, such as Scripture and its proper interpretation, were taken up in preceding chapters. The following topics were chosen because, among others, they play a very important role in the study and interpretation of Biblical theology.

A. Christology

Aside from properly defining the true nature of Scripture and its authority, the proper Biblical understanding of Christology is of utmost importance, as the Scriptures emphasize again and again. This involves a careful study of the gospels and the epistles in their proper historical and theological context along with the prophecies of the Old Testament. The titles listed below under both Christology and the gospels supplement those listed for the study of the Old and New Testament in earlier chapters.

Among the many titles one might list, the following are perhaps the most helpful. The bibliographies included in these titles list many other resources.

Beasley-Murray, George R. *Jesus and the Kingdom.* Grand Rapids, MI: Eerdmans, 1986.
Divides his study into three parts: I. the coming of God in the Old Testament; II. the coming of God in the writings of early Judaism; III. the coming of God in the teachings of Jesus. Includes a broad spectrum of varying views of Biblical scholarship.
Bruce, F. F. *New Testament Development of Old Testament Themes.* Grand Rapids, MI: Eerdmans, 1968.

A study of Old Testament passages and their fulfillment in the New Testament under selected categories.

Cullmann, Oscar. *The Christology of the New Testament*. Rev. ed. Philadelphia: Westminster, 1963.

A standard title by a member of the "salvation history" school.

France, R. T. *Jesus and the Old Testament: His Application of Old Testament Passages to Himself and His Mission*. Downers Grove, IL: InterVarsity, 1971.

Green, Michael. *The Empty Cross of Jesus*. Downers Grove, IL: InterVarsity, 1984.

Looks at the crucial importance of the cross and the empty tomb in the light of Scripture; and their significance for the theologian, preacher, counselor, disciple, and for the destiny of humanity generally.

Gunton, Colin E. *Yesterday & Today: A Study of Continuities in Christology*. Grand Rapids, MI: Eerdmans, 1983.

A study of the form, content, and method in Christology. He addresses the distinctively modern context of so-called Christological problems in the light of ancient and modern approaches to Christology.

Harris, Murray J. *Raised Immortal: Resurrection and Immortality in the New Testament*. Grand Rapids, MI: Eerdmans, 1983.

Part I studies the resurrection of Christ and that of the believers. Part II discusses immortality and the relationship between resurrection and immortality.

Hengel, Martin. *The Atonement: The Origins of the Doctrine in the New Testament*. Philadelphia: Fortress, 1981.

Begins with a study of atonement in classical antiquity and then traces this doctrine through the New Testament.

—————. *The Son of God: The Origin of Christology and the History of Jewish-Hellenistic Religion*. Philadelphia: Fortress, 1976.

Investigates various hypotheses of the "history of religions school" and ancient Judaism in the light of Scripture, and especially of Paul and the Letter to the Hebrews.

Kim, Seyoon. *The Son of Man as the Son of God*. Grand Rapids, MI: Eerdmans, 1985.

A careful study of Jesus' self-designation as the "Son of Man," its meaning and significance in the light of the witness of Scripture.

Longenecker, Richard N. *The Christology of Early Jewish Christianity.* Grand Rapids, MI: Baker, 1970.

A valuable study of Christology as found in Scripture and pertinent references in intertestamental and early rabbinic writings.

Marshall, I. Howard. *The Origins of New Testament Christology.* Issues in Contemporary Theology. Downers Grove, IL: InterVarsity, 1976.

In his study, Marshall carefully draws on the Scriptures and also surveys some of the dominant critical hypotheses.

Morris, Leon. *The Atonement: Its Meaning and Significance.* Grand Rapids, MI: Zondervan, 1983.

In the light of Scripture Morris looks at such crucial terms as covenant, justification, propitiation, reconciliation, and sacrifice and their decisive implications for salvation.

————. *The Apostolic Preaching of the Cross.* 3rd ed. Grand Rapids, MI: Eerdmans, 1965.

A careful study of the Greek and Hebrew terms used in Scripture for Christ's vicarious atonement and their significance for the salvation of sinful humanity.

————. *The Cross in the New Testament.* Grand Rapids, MI: Eerdmans, 1965.

A valuable study of the crucial importance of the cross in the New Testament. Includes a special chapter on the cross in Hebrews.

Runia, Klaas. *The Present-Day Christological Debate.* Downers Grove, IL: InterVarsity, 1984.

Runia discusses the central emphases of John Robinson, Hans Kueng, E. Schillebeeckx, Juergen Moltmann, and W. Pannenberg in the light of the apostolic faith as found in Scripture.

Schaller, John. *Biblical Christology: A Study in Lutheran Dogmatics.* Milwaukee: Northwestern, 1981.

A penetrating study in the language of systematics of the total span of the Biblical doctrine of Christology.

Stott, John R. W. *The Cross of Christ.* Downers Grove, IL: InterVarsity, 1986.

Stott takes up the meaning and significance of the cross in four parts: I. approaching the cross; II. the heart of the cross; III. the achievement of the cross; IV. living under the cross. An extensive bibliography is included.

Wenham, John. *Easter Enigma: Are the Resurrection Accounts in Conflict?* Downers Grove, IL: InterVarsity, 1984.

Wenham takes the Easter narratives and shows how they come together into a historical sequence.

B. The Gospels

Bright, John. *The Kingdom of God: The Biblical Concept and Its Meaning for the Church.* Nashville: Abingdon, 1953.

A standard title on the unifying theme of covenant (kingdom of God) in the Scriptures and its implications for each age and for today. Reflects some critical categories.

Carson, Donald. *The Sermon on the Mount: An Evangelical Exposition of Matthew 5–7.* Grand Rapids, MI: Baker, 1978.

A careful exposition of the Sermon on the Mount in non-technical language, emphasizing the meaning and implications throughout of *makarioi.*

Farmer, William R. *The Synoptic Problem: A Critical Analysis.* Dillsboro, NC: Western North Carolina Press, 1976.

Documents how the hypothetical Markan priority came into being, despite the witness of history that Matthew was the first gospel written.

Hengel, Martin. *Crucifixion in the Ancient World and the Folly of the Message of the Cross.* Philadelphia: Fortress, 1977.

A study of crucifixion, its practice by various peoples in history, and the meaning of 1 Corinthians 1:18.

Jeremias, Joachim. *Jerusalem in the Time of Jesus.* Philadelphia: Fortress, 1975.

A magisterial investigation into the economic, social, and religious conditions in New Testament Jerusalem. Documents the crucial role played by the temple and its hierarchy in the total life of Jerusalem.

Manson, T. W. *The Servant-Messiah: A Study of the Public Ministry of Jesus.* Grand Rapids, MI: Baker, 1961.

Drawing on intertestamental apocalyptic literature, the author demonstrates the decisive influence of the Jewish messianic expectation on the life and thought of Jesus' hearers, who were unable to listen to Jesus in terms of His message in the light of Scripture.

Marshall, I. Howard. *Last Supper and Lord's Supper.* Grand Rapids, MI: Eerdmans, 1980.

A valuable study by an evangelical scholar. Looks at some of the novel hypotheses proposed for the Passover meal Jesus ate with His disciples, the significance of the Lord's Supper and its observance in the early church.

Sherwin-White, A. N. *Roman Society and Roman Law in the New Testament.* Grand Rapids, MI: Baker, 1963.

An invaluable study by a famous Oxford classicist who stresses the crucial importance of the light shed by the New Testament and especially by Luke on life and legal procedures of the first century.

C. Parables

Parables form one-third of the contents of the gospels. Unfortunately the parables, their true nature and proper interpretation, are too often misunderstood and misapplied. It is essential that every parable be carefully heard for its "then and there" meaning before seeking to ascertain its "here and now" meaning. The following are the most helpful resources on parables. Not included are titles which follow an existential approach, regarding the parables as "language events" regardless of their setting and meaning within the ministry of Jesus and the message He sought to convey.

Bailey, Kenneth E. *The Poet and Peasant—Through Peasant Eyes.* 2 vols. in 1. Grand Rapids, MI: Eerdmans, 1984.

An invaluable literary and cultural study of parables in Luke by a Biblical scholar who has spent most of his life in the Near East and who, on the basis of careful criteria, helps the reader to "hear" the parables in their total context as Jesus' hearers heard them.

Jeremias, Joachim. *The Parables of Jesus.* 2nd rev. ed. New York: Scribners, 1972.

A helpful study of the parables by a famous Biblical scholar who spent some years in Palestine. Following his form critical approach, Jeremias seeks to find "the very words of Jesus."

Scharlemann, Martin H. *Proclaiming the Parables.* St. Louis: Concordia, 1963.

A primary resource for the study of parables and their proper interpretation within their setting. Discusses their meaning and implications for life within the kingdom of God. Shows how to arrive at the single point of comparison and its significance for reaching the central spiritual truth in each parable.

Stein, Robert H. *An Introduction to the Parables of Jesus.* Philadelphia: Westminster, 1981.

Looks at the what and why of Jesus' parables within the framework of the kingdom of God. Traces the history of the study of parables and the critical presuppositions often used today. Suggests basic principles for studying parables and how to apply them.

D. Pauline Studies

A great theologian once said that the apostle Paul was the greatest mind in the New Testament and was mightily used by God to interpret with infinite care the person and the work of Jesus and His decisive significance for the salvation of humanity.

The following selected bibliography represents some of the most helpful of the large number of resources in this category.

Barclay, William. *The Mind of St. Paul.* New York: Harper & Row, 1975.

A stimulating overview of St. Paul, his life and mindset prior to and after his conversion, as well as highlights of his theology as reflected in his epistles.

Bruce, F. F. *Paul: Apostle of the Heart Set Free.* Grand Rapids, MI: Eerdmans, 1977.

A careful study of the apostle Paul, his life and thought, on the basis of Acts and his epistles and within the total context of the first-century world.

Davies, W. D. *Paul and Rabbinic Judaism: Some Rabbinic Elements in Pauline Theology.* 4th ed. Philadelphia: Fortress, 1980.

A classic, indispensable resource for a study of Paul's theology, with careful attention to aspects of first-century Judaism as this is reflected in Paul's background and writing.

Ellis, E. Earle. *Paul's Use of the Old Testament.* Grand Rapids, MI: Baker, 1985 reprint.

Investigates the rationale of Paul's use of the Old Testament in his sermons and letters. A valuable resource.

Johnson, Kent L. *Paul the Teacher: A Resource for Teachers in the Church.* Minneapolis: Augsburg, 1986.

A study of Paul's epistles underscores that Paul was one of the great teachers of all time. This is carefully documented and demonstrated in this valuable resource.

Kim, Seyoon. *The Origin of Paul's Gospel.* Grand Rapids, MI: Eerdmans, 1982.

In contrast to the variety of hypothetical origins posited by some today, Kim sees Christ's appearance to Paul on the Damascus Road as decisively crucial and as the source of his theology, which is then reflected in his total ministry and letters.

Ridderbos, Herman. *Paul: An Outline of His Theology.* Grand Rapids, MI: Eerdmans, 1975.

One of the recent important studies of the apostle Paul and his theology, worthy of careful and discerning study.

Schoeps, Hans Joachim. *Paul: The Theology of the Apostle in the Light of Jewish Religious History.* Philadelphia: Westminster, 1961.

A standard title in Pauline studies by a distinguished Jewish scholar.

Whiteley, D. E. H. *The Theology of St. Paul.* 2nd ed. Oxford: Basil Blackwell, 1985 reprint.

A standard resource which looks at the background of Paul's theology, the created order, the fall and its results, preparation for the Gospel, "the Lord and the Spirit," the whole work of Christ, how Christ's work affects humanity, church and ministry, morality, and eschatology.

XII

Judaica

A. Jewish Apocalyptic and Pseudepigrapha

The discoveries at Qumran have resulted in an intensified interest in and investigation of Jewish writings of the intertestamental period, also as more of these have come to light. This has led to a greater appreciation of the decisive importance of these documents for a better understanding of the late centuries B.C. and of the pre- and post-A.D. 70 periods.

The following is a selection of writings on Jewish apocalyptic and pseudepigrapha and their place in Biblical studies:

Charlesworth, James H., ed. *The Old Testament Pseudepigrapha.* Garden City, NY: Doubleday, Vol. 1, 1983; Vol. 2, 1984.

This title brings up-to-date the two-volume edition of 1913 edited by R. H. Charles. Aside from general articles, each of the documents is preceded by an introductory article by the translator together with annotated footnotes accompanying the translation. This is a monumental work and of great importance for Biblical studies.

Collins, John J. *Between Athens and Jerusalem: Jewish Identity in the Hellenistic Diaspora.* New York: Crossroad, 1983.

An insightful analysis of the encounter of Hellenism and the Hebrew faith in the Jewish diaspora, particularly in the Hellenized civilization of Egypt.

Maier, Johann. *The Temple Scroll: An Introduction, Translation & Commentary.* Journal for the Study of the Old Testament Supplement Series 34. Sheffield, England: JSOT Press, 1985.

McNamara, Martin. *Palestinian Judaism and the New Testament.* Good News Studies 4. Wilmington, DE: Michael Glazier, 1983.

Basically an introduction to several types of Jewish literature and their importance for New Testament studies, written for the non-specialist. Operates with the supposition that many targum traditions are early in origin; this is a matter of dispute among specialists.

Metzger, Bruce M., ed. *The Oxford Annotated Apocrypha of the Old Testament Revised Standard Version*. New York: Oxford, 1965.

A valuable resource with an overall introduction, and introductory articles on each book, together with annotations.

Nickelsburg, George W. E. *Jewish Literature Between the Bible and the Mishnah: A Historical and Literary Introduction*. Philadelphia: Fortress, 1981.

A valuable resource which seeks systematically to relate the literature to the historical periods in which it took shape and attempts to show how the various Jewish writers faced the problems of their age.

————. *Resurrection, Immortality, and Eternal Life in Intertestamental Judaism*. Harvard Theological Studies XXXVI. Cambridge, MS: Harvard University Press, 1972.

A standard title on the above subject area.

Nickelsburg, George W. E., and Michael E. Stone. *Faith and Piety in Early Judaism: Texts and Documents*. Philadelphia: Fortress, 1983.

Drawing on Scripture, apocrypha, pseudepigrapha, Qumran, and other documents, the authors show how patterns of faith and piety influenced Jewish religious thought and life.

Rost, Leonhard. *Judaism Outside the Hebrew Canon: An Introduction to the Documents*. Nashville: Abingdon, 1971.

An invaluable authoritative resource of succinct information on the apocrypha and the pseudepigrapha.

Russell, D. S. *Apocalyptic: Ancient and Modern*. Philadelphia: Fortress, 1978.

Surveys apocalyptic in the Old Testament and the noncanonical literature, and indicates how these in part are reflected in the New Testament.

————. *Between the Testaments*. Philadelphia: Fortress, 1960.

A very helpful survey of the history, life, and apocalyptic thought patterns in Judaism, and the effect of these on Jewish messianic expectations in the first century.

———. *The Method and Message of Jewish Apocalyptic 200 B.C.–A.D. 100*. Philadelphia: Westminster, 1964.

A masterful study of Jewish apocalyptic, its nature, identity, method, and message.

———. *From Early Judaism to Early Church*. Philadelphia: Fortress, 1986.

Takes up such matters as the cultural and religious developments in the Hellenistic age, the sources and Scripture, Biblical interpretation in early Judaism and in the New Testament, the Torah, prayer and meditation, demonology and evil, the Jewish apocalyptic and the future hope.

Stone, Michael E., ed. *Jewish Writings of the Second Temple Period: Apocrypha, Pseudepigrapha, Qumran Sectarian Writings, Philo, Josephus*. Philadelphia: Fortress, 1984. Vol. 2 of *The Literature of the Jewish People in the Period of the Second Temple and the Talmud*.

Contributors include George Nickelsburg, H. Attridge, Peter Borgen, M. Gilbert, John Collins, B. Pearson, M. Dimant, David Flusser, and P. Alexander.

———. *Scriptures, Sects and Visions: A Profile of Judaism from Ezra to the Jewish Revolts*. Philadelphia: Fortress, 1980.

Basically integrates the important manuscript finds of the past decades into a fresh picture of intertestamental Judaism.

B. Jewish History and Interpretation

The literature in this area has been growing considerably in recent years. The matter of seeking to ascertain the Judaism of the first century is a matter of much interest as well as much disagreement among specialists. This is reflected also in the selected titles listed below. Unfortunately some very valuable studies are no longer in print.

Bowker, John. *The Targums and Rabbinic Literature: An Introduction to Jewish Interpretation of Scripture*. New York: Cambridge University Press, 1969.

Divided into two parts: the background of the targums, and a study of the Pseudo-Jonathon together with annotations and appendixes.

Chilton, Bruce D. *A Galilean Rabbi and His Bible: Jesus' Use of the Interpreted Scripture of His Time.* Good News Studies 8. Wilmington, DE: Michael Glazier, 1984.

Begins with an overview of Judaism and research in targums and early Judaism. Seeks to apply this in a study of Jesus and parallels seen in the targum to Isaiah. Comments on Jesus' style of preaching on Scripture as fulfilled. Some critical overtones evident.

Danby, Herbert. *The Mishnah.* New York: Oxford University Press, 1954.

The standard translation of the Mishnah, dating back to ca. A.D. 220.

Daube, David. *The New Testament and Rabbinic Judaism.* Salem, NH: Ayer Co., 1973 reprint.

A standard title by a famous scholar of Judaica. Takes up messianic titles, legislative and narrative forms, concepts and conventions. A valuable resource.

France, R. T., and David Wenham, eds. *Studies in Midrash and Historiography.* Sheffield, England: JSOT Press, 1983.

Green, Michael S., ed. *Approaches to Ancient Judaism. Volume V. Studies in Judaism and Its Greco-Roman Context.* Brown Judaic Studies 32. Decatur, GA: Scholars Press, 1985.

A valuable collection of 10 essays on, for example, religion in Athens, Rome, and Jerusalem in the last century B.C., Jewish rights in Greek cities under Roman rule, Galilean regionalism, and the study of early Christianity.

Hengel, Martin. *Jews, Greeks and Barbarians: Aspects of the Hellenization of Judaism in the pre-Christian Period.* Philadelphia: Fortress, 1980.

A careful study of the effect of Hellenization in Palestine and in the Diaspora by a highly respected scholar of Judaism.

——— . *Judaism and Hellenism: Studies in Their Encounter in Palestine during the Early Hellenistic Period.* 2nd ed. 2 vols. in 1. Philadelphia: Fortress, 1974.

An exhaustive survey of early Hellenism as a political, economic, and cultural force; the conflict between Palestinian Judaism and the spirit of the Hellenistic age, and the Hellenistic reform attempt in Jerusalem. Very extensive notes, bibliographies, and indexes.

Jeremias, Joachim. *Jerusalem in the Time of Jesus: An Investigation into Economic and Social Conditions during the New Testament Period*. Philadelphia: Fortress, 1969.

A careful investigation of economic conditions, social status, and the maintenance of racial purity in Jerusalem in Jesus' time.

Kraft, Robert A., and George W. E. Nickelsburg, eds. *Early Judaism and Its Modern Interpreters*. Philadelphia: Fortress and Atlanta: Scholars Press, 1986.

The work of selected specialists in Judaica, the subject-matter is divided into three parts: I. early Judaism in its historical settings; II. recent discoveries; III. the literature.

Neusner, Jacob. *From Politics to Piety: The Emergence of Pharisaic Judaism*. Englewood Cliffs, NJ: Prentice-Hall, 1973.

Presents his specific view of the Pharisees: their origins, Hillel, the gospels' portrayal, and rabbinical traditions.

————. *Judaism in the Beginning of Christianity*. Philadelphia: Fortress, 1984.

An overview of the world of Jesus' time, three types of Judaism in the first century, the Pharisees and Hillel, and the effect of Jerusalem's destruction on Judaism.

Safrai, S., and M. Stern, eds. *The Jewish People in the First Century: Historical Geography, Political History, Social, Cultural and Religious Life and Institutions*. Philadelphia: Fortress, Vol. 1, 1974; Vol. 2, 1976; Section 2:2, 1984.

A massive, up-to-date study by an international team of scholars designed to survey the history of the relationship between Judaism and Christianity in the early centuries A.D. The last title centers on the apocrypha, pseudepigrapha, Qumran sectarian writings, Philo, and Josephus.

Schuerer, E. *The History of the Jewish People in the Age of Jesus Christ (175 B.C.–A.D. 135)*. Rev. ed. G. Vermes and F. Millar. Edinburgh: T. & T. Clark, Vol. 1, 1973; Vol. 2, 1979; Vol. 3, Part I, 1986.

Volume 1 surveys Palestine's history through the Seleucid, Hasmonean, and Roman periods to A.D. 135. Volume 2 looks at the cultural, political, and religious institutions and messianism. Volume 3, Part I, takes up Judaism in the dispersion and the non-canonical Jewish literature, including Qumran. Volume 3, Part

II, will discuss Jewish literature of which the original language is uncertain.

Stone, Michael E. *Scriptures, Sects and Visions: A Profile of Judaism from Ezra to the Jewish Revolts.* Philadelphia: Fortress, 1980.
Integrates recent finds into a fresh picture of intertestamental Judaism: its varieties, its contacts with other religions, and the influence of the apocalyptic.

Tcherikover, Victor. *Hellenistic Civilization and the Jews.* Philadelphia: Jewish Publication Society of America, 1959.
A standard title by a specialist. A study of Hellenistic civilization in Palestine and in the dispersion.

XIII

Geographical Resources and Atlases

A. Biblical Geography

1. The Importance of Biblical Geography

Bible history and theology are deeply rooted in geography. The Biblical events took place in a specific geographical setting, and this must be recognized to understand properly each historical event.

The history of God's covenant people was deeply influenced by the history of the surrounding nations of the Near East. The land of Canaan was the central span of the great land bridge of the Near East, connecting Egypt in the southwest with the nations to the north, the northwest, and the northeast. In the earlier period this included the Hittites, and later the powers of Mesopotamia: Assyria, Babylon, and Persia. Not to be overlooked were the smaller nations adjoining the land of ancient Israel: Phoenicia, Syria, Ammon, Moab, and Edom.

Important roads of trade and commerce crossed this great land bridge. The famous Way of the Sea *(Via Maris)* linked Egypt with the nations to the north. It entered the land of Canaan in the area of Gaza, traversed the coastal plain, wound its way through the Megiddo pass of the Carmel range across the Esdraelon Plain into Lower Galilee, and crossed the Upper Jordan River north of the Sea of Galilee near Hazor on its way to Damascus and points north.

Another important avenue of trade, the King's Highway, went south from Damascus east of the Jordan and the Dead Sea into the

Arabah to the Gulf of Aqaba. Roads running east and west intersected and connected these arteries. The control of these great trade highways played an important role in Biblical history.

The land of Canaan (later, Palestine) was a small area, approximately 150 miles from Dan to Beersheba and about 54 miles from Gaza to the Dead Sea and 28 miles from Accho (later, Ptolemais) to the Sea of Galilee. The coastline itself is less than 75 miles from the great Arabian Desert to the east. But in this comparatively small area was a vast variety of geography, topography, variations in climate and fertility, as well as coveted natural resources. All these features made this land highly desirable, and they play an intimate role in a proper study of Biblical history.

A scientific approach to Biblical geography is relatively recent, since it is very closely related to Biblical archaeology. Perhaps the most important ancient resource is the *Onomaticon* prepared by the church father Eusebius of Caesarea (ca. 260–ca. 340). This is an indispensable resource for the scholar.

In 1838 Edward Robinson and Eli Smith began a study of Palestine west of the Jordan on horseback. They visited site after site, checked out possible identifications, and mapped their travels. The result of their work, published as *Biblical Researches in Palestine* (2nd ed. 3 vols. Boston: Crocker and Brewster, 1860) is still valuable today. Many of their identifications are still recognized as being correct. Their work was also foundational for ongoing geographical research today.

In 1865 the Palestine Exploration Fund was founded in England. This was followed by the founding of the Deutscher Palaestina Verein, the American School of Oriental Research, and the Ecole Biblique de St. Etienne in Jerusalem by the French Dominicans, and the Israel Exploration Society in more recent years. All these have made tremendous contributions to the advancement of geographical, archaeological, and historical knowledge.

Of great importance was the monumental work of H. H. Kitchen and C. R. Conder of the Palestine Exploration Fund, who made a careful survey of Western Palestine (*The Survey of Western Palestine*, 3 vols. London, 1881–83). Their excellent maps are one of their great legacies, serving as the model for maps of this region today. Hermann Gute of the Deutscher Palaestina Verein also made a very helpful contribution.

2. Selected Bibliography

Unfortunately some excellent titles of the past are no longer published today. Among them is the stellar work by Denis Baly, *The Geography of the Bible* (Rev. ed. New York: Harper & Row, 1978).

Aharoni, Yohanan. *The Land of the Bible: A Historical Geography of the Bible.* Trans. A. F. Rainey. 2nd. ed. Philadelphia: Westminster, 1979.

Based on the latest archaeological research at the time of printing. Covers the Old Testament period. The reader needs to remember that the exact location of some sites mentioned in history may not as yet be established archaeologically.

Avi-Yonah, Michael. *The Holy Land, From the Persian to the Arab Conquest (536 B.C. to A.D. 640).* Trans. A. F. Rainey. Rev. ed. Grand Rapids, MI: Baker, n.d.

Baly, Denis. *Basic Biblical Geography.* Philadelphia: Fortress, 1987.

A concise, comprehensive overview of the geography of Palestine and Transjordan by a trained geographer and Bible scholar who lived in the Middle East for many years. Included are photographs, illustrations and maps. Valuable resource.

Pfeiffer, C. F., and H. F. Vos. *Wycliffe Historical Geography of Bible Lands.* Chicago: Moody, 1967.

Seeks to be faithful to Scripture and history. Illustrated.

Smith, George Adam. *The Historical Geography of the Holy Land.* London: Collins, 1974. Paperback.

A reprint of an old classic, graphic in description.

Van Der Woude, A. S. ed. *The World of the Bible.* Grand Rapids, MI: Eerdmans, 1986.

Begins his study with a succinct overview of the geography of the Bible lands. Also includes information on archaeology, writing and the text of the Scriptures, as well as Biblical institutions. Illustrated. A valuable resource.

Zohary, Michael. *Plants of the Bible.* New York: Cambridge University Press, 1982.

A complete handbook to all the plants of the Bible with 200 color plates, prepared by one of the foremost botanists in Israel. Also a glossary and index to Biblical references.

B. Bible Atlases

1. Importance

A good Bible atlas is an indispensable tool for purposeful Bible study. Such an atlas is deeply indebted to George Adam Smith's classic *Historical Atlas of the Holy Land* (London: Hodder and Stoughton, 1936). This title together with his book listed above is still an important resource, even though recent archaeological investigation has shed much light on the location of certain sites. Also an important title of the past is Pere F. M. Abel's *Geographie de la Palestine* (Paris: Librairie Lecoffre, Vol. I, 1933; Vol. II, 1938). Aside from political and historical geography, Abel also includes climate, fauna, flora, geology, hydrology, and mineralogy.

A well-done atlas includes the names of rivers, mountains, and geographical regions. Although not every town may be included, it should identify towns that played a significant role in Bible history. It should also feature geographical contours in clear, accurate relief. Major trade routes should be indicated on maps. It should feature charts and ideally also maps providing information on rainfall. Some atlases also include temperature charts of various parts of Palestine during the year. Finally, the atlas should include an accurate index of sites and geographical features. Obviously, all such information should be based on the latest available research.

2. Selected Bibliography

Aharoni, Y., and M. Avi-Yonah. *The Macmillan Bible Atlas.* Rev. ed. New York: Macmillan, 1977.

In a series of two-color maps, covers Biblical history and includes the defeat of Bar Kochba in A.D. 135. Follows late dating from patriarchs through the time of Samuel. Helpful period maps plus historical description of the period.

Beitzel, Barry J. *The Moody Atlas of Bible Lands.* Chicago: Moody, 1985.

Divided into three parts: I. the physical geography of the Holy Land; II. the historical geography of the Holy Land; III. the history of Biblical mapmaking. Part II traces the various periods of Biblical history in a series of maps. Features many color pictures.

Blaiklock, E. M., ed. *The Zondervan Pictorial Bible Atlas*. Grand Rapids, MI: Zondervan, 1972.

Features nine full-color maps from an earlier Rand McNally collection plus 68 one-color maps; also 16 chapters of text on the history, geography, climate and other features of the area.

Bruce, F. F. *Bible History Atlas: Popular Study Edition*. New York: Crossroad, 1982.

Designed for the beginner, very simple in its approach to content.

Gardner, Joseph L. *Reader's Digest Atlas of the Bible*. Pleasantville, NY: Reader's Digest Association, 1981.

Combines maps, pictures, and descriptive copy for the interested student of the Bible.

May, Herbert G., ed. *Oxford Bible Atlas*. 3rd ed. Rev. John Day. New York: Oxford University Press, 1984.

One of the best of Bible atlases. Features well-done, easy-to-read maps together with a summary of history and extensive gazetteer. Available in either hardbound or paperback.

Monson, John, consultant. *Student Map Manual: Historical Geography of the Bible Lands*. Grand Rapids, MI: Zondervan, 1979.

Perhaps the most innovative atlas with maps in horizontal rather than vertical format. Much helpful copy.

Pfeiffer, C. F. *Baker's Bible Atlas*. Rev. ed. Grand Rapids, MI: Baker, 1961.

Maps, black-white pictures, pertinent copy, and a quick overview of Biblical archaeology.

Rogerson, John. *Atlas of the Bible*. New York: Facts on File, 1985.

A highly illustrated resource covering the Bible, its literature, history, and geography. Some critical overtones.

Wright, G. Ernest, and Floyd V. Filson. *Westminster Historical Atlas to the Bible*. Rev. ed. Philadelphia: Westminster, 1956.

Carefully written descriptive copy. The topographical coloring of the maps fails to give a clear picture. The size of the atlas makes desk use somewhat awkward.

XIV

Archaeology

A. Survey of Development

Archaeology may be defined as "the scientific study of material remains of human life and activities in the past." Its purpose is to see how men and women lived in the past and to appreciate the light that such a study sheds on human history. This requires careful planning and organization before an archaeological excavation is begun. It also requires careful, systematic recovery and a discerning analysis and interpretation of all that is found.

Biblical archaeology falls into two phases. The first phase was ushered in with Napolean's invasion of Egypt in 1798 and closed with World War I. The second phase began after this war and continues into the present.

Among the great pioneers in the first phase were men such as the pioneer Egyptologist Francois Champollion, the great Assyriologist Henry C. Rawlinson, James Henry Breasted—the founder of the Oriental Institute at the University of Chicago, and Heinrich Schliemann, the excavator of Homer's Troy. Sir William Ramsay's researches in Turkey shed much light on sites and events recorded in the Book of Acts. John Garstang's archaeological activity to learn more about the history of the Hittites, facets of Egyptian life and history, as well as his excavations at Jericho and in Palestine merit careful study. Important also were the geographical researches of men like Edward Robinson and Eli Smith in Palestine and adjacent regions, beginning in 1836.

Tremendous strides forward in methodology, techniques, recording and analysis of data, as well as in other areas have been made since World War I. Among the many who made great contributions to Biblical archaeology in Palestine and the immediate countries are William Foxwell Albright, Nelson Glueck, Mortimer Wheeler, Kathleen M. Kenyon, Roland DeVaux, Claude F. A. Schaeffer, G. Ernest Wright, James B. Pritchard, G. Lankester Harding, Yigael Yadin, and Yohanan Aharoni.

Recent years have seen a widening divergency of opinion whether to continue to speak of Biblical archaeology or Syro-Palestinian archaeology. Involved in this new view are critical presuppositions with special reference to the historicity of the exodus account and its implications for Israel's early history.

Presently the term promoted by some is "New Biblical Archaeology." This envisions, as one proponent stated, a dialog between the emphasis on archaeology and "the best of current Biblical scholarship." In essence, this means giving decisive validity to the various critical approaches to the Old Testament, and especially to their views on Israel's early history. In time, the suggested term, "New Biblical Archaeology," would give way to Syro-Palestinian archaeology. The archaeological data apart from the Biblical text would seemingly be viewed as primary and decisive.

B. Selected Bibliography

1. Methodology

Recent years have seen careful refinement of excavation methodology and procedures. Some excavators have developed techniques so that all data on artifacts can be computerized to facilitate organization and study of this crucial data in preparation for reporting the results of the excavation. The following are among the latest titles on methodology:

Blakely, J. A., L. E. Toombs, and K. G. O'Donnell, eds. *The Tell El-Hesi Field Manual.* Cambridge: American Schools of Oriental Research, 1980.

Dever, W. G., and H. D. Lance, eds. *A Manual of Field Excavation.* New York: KTAV, 1979.

Joukowsky, Martha. *A Complete Manual of Field Archaeology: Tools and Techniques of Field Work for Archaeology.* Englewood Cliffs, NJ: Prentice-Hall, 1980.

2. Overview of Archaeology

The following is a selection of many titles available on archaeological activity in Bible lands and the light such activity sheds for purposeful Bible study. A growing number of titles are becoming available on individual sites and areas, for example, a series being published by Eerdmans. As one would expect, each year some titles go out of print and other titles are added.

Aharoni, Yohanan. *The Archaeology of the Land of Israel.* Tr. Anson F. Rainey. Philadelphia: Westminster, 1978.

After a quick geographical introduction, Aharoni discusses material on the prehistoric, chalcolithic, Canaanite, and Israelite periods. Many figures, plates, and photographs together with a listing of flint tools and pottery.

Albright, William F. *Archaeology and the Religion of Israel.* 5th ed. Baltimore: Johns Hopkins University Press, 1968.

————. *The Archaeology of Palestine.* Rev. ed. Gloucester, MA: Peter Smith, 1971.

————. *From the Stone Age to Christianity.* 2nd ed. Baltimore: Johns Hopkins University Press, 1957.

Avigad, Nahman. *Discovering Jerusalem.* Nashville: Nelson, 1980.

Professor Avigad reports on the results of his extensive excavations in the Jewish Quarter of the Old City, which sheds much light especially on the first century A.D. and the destruction of Jerusalem by the Romans in A.D. 70. Well illustrated.

Avi-Yonah, Michael, ed. *Encyclopedia of Archaeological Excavations in the Holy Land.* Jerusalem: The Israel Exploration Society and Masada Press, Vol. 1, 1975; Vol. 2, 1976; Vol. 3, 1977; Vol. 4, 1978.

A beautifully illustrated resource prepared by a number of Israeli scholars under the English editorship of Dr. Avi-Yonah and, beginning with Volume 3, Ephraim Stern. It presents the latest information as of the date of publication. The sites are arranged in alphabetical order.

Baez-Camargo, Gonzalo. *Archaeological Commentary on the Bible.* New York: Doubleday, 1984.

Blaiklock, E. M. *The Archaeology of the New Testament.* Rev. ed. Nashville: Nelson, 1984.

————. *The New International Dictionary of Biblical Archaeology.* Grand Rapids, MI: Zondervan, 1983.

Davies, Graham I., ed. *Cities of the Biblical World.* Guilford, England: Lutterworth Press.

A series of studies on selected cities and towns with illustrations and maps. Presently studies on four have been released.

Dowley, Tim, ed. *Discovering the Bible: Archaeologists Look at Scripture.* Grand Rapids, MI: Eerdmans, 1986.

A beautifully planned and executed resource by practicing archaeologists on sites and aspects of life in the Biblical world. Highly illustrated with color photographs, reconstructions, and maps.

Finegan, Jack. *Archaeological History of the Ancient Middle East.* Boulder, CO: Westview Press, 1979.

————. *The Archaeology of the New Testament: The Life and the Beginning of the Early Church.* Princeton, NJ: Princeton University Press, 1970.

Heavily illustrated description of Jesus' life and ministry, beginning with John the Baptist through Jesus' ascension.

————. *The Archaeology of the New Testament: The Mediterranean World of the Early Christian Apostles.* Boulder, CO: Westview Press, 1981.

Heavily illustrated description of the activity of Paul, Peter, and John.

Harrison, R. K. *Major Cities of the Biblical World.* Nashville: Nelson, 1985.

Treatment of the cities arranged in alphabetical order with maps and pictures. Material uneven in quality. Especially useful for the nonspecialist.

Keel, Othmar. *The Symbolism of the Biblical World.* New York: Seabury, 1978.

Features pictures of statues, symbols, and other archaeological illustrations with descriptions of their significance for Biblical study.

Kenyon, Kathleen. *Archaeology in the Holy Land.* 4th ed. Nashville: Nelson, 1985.

————. *The Bible and Recent Archaeology.* Atlanta: John Knox, 1979.

Kitchen, Kenneth A. *The Ancient Orient and the Old Testament.* Downers Grove, IL: InterVarsity, 1966.

A survey of archaeological finds and their significance.

Lance, Darrell. *The Old Testament and the Archaeologist.* Philadelphia: Fortress, 1981.

Meyers, E. M., and J. F. Strange, *Archaeology, the Rabbis, and Early Christianity: The Social and Historical Setting of Palestinian Judaism and Christianity.* Nashville: Abingdon, 1981.

Pritchard, James B., ed. *The Ancient Near East: An Anthology of Texts and Pictures.* Princeton, NJ: Princeton University Press, Vol. I, 1973; Vol. II, 1975.

Translation of ancient texts of the Old Testament era together with pictures of sites, statues, and artifacts.

Schoville, Keith N. *Biblical Archaeology in Focus.* Grand Rapids, MI: Eerdmans, 1978.

A significant title divided into three parts: understanding Biblical archaeology; a survey of significant sites and finds outside the Holy Land; and a similar survey of sites within the Holy Land.

Shanks, Herschel, and Benjamin Mazar. *Recent Archaeology in the Land of Israel.* Washington, DC: Biblical Archaeological Society, 1985.

A series of articles by Israeli scholars on archaeological activity in Israel. Includes recent archaeological research in Jerusalem.

Thompson, James A. *The Bible and Archaeology.* 3rd ed. Grand Rapids, MI: Eerdmans, 1982.

Vos, Howard F. *Archaeology in Bible Lands.* Chicago: Moody, 1972.

————. *Introduction to Biblical Archaeology.* Chicago: Moody, 1983.

Wiseman, Donald J., and Edwin Yamauchi. *Archaeology and the Bible.* Grand Rapids, MI: Zondervan, 1979.

Wright, G. Ernest. *Biblical Archaeology.* Rev. ed. Philadelphia: Westminster, 1963.

XV

Culture and Society

Recent decades have seen the publication of much helpful material on the total setting of the life and history of the Scriptures. To be acquainted with these is of great importance if one is to understand more fully a given period, event, or passage. The following are selected titles from the mass of materials available under several headings.

A. "Daily Life"

Bouquet, A. C. *Everyday Life in New Testament Times.* New York: Scribners, 1954.
An illustrated study of daily life in New Testament times.

Casson, Lionel. *Ships and Seamanship in the Ancient World.* Princeton, NJ: Princeton University Press, 1986.
A reprint of an earlier work with a new appendix by one of the world's authorities on maritime activities in the ancient world.

Grosvenor, Gilbert, ed. *Everyday Life in Ancient Times.* Washington, DC: National Geographic Society, 1961.
A beautifully illustrated presentation of life in ancient Mesopotamia, Egypt, Greece, and Rome.

Heaton, E. W. *Everyday Life in Old Testament Times.* New York: Scribners, 1977.
An illustrated study of daily life in Old Testament times.

Klinck, Arthur W. *Home Life in Bible Times: A Study in Biblical Antiquities.* St. Louis: Concordia, 1947.
An illustrated study of daily life in the Biblical era.

Miller, Madeleine S., J. Lane Miller, Boyce M. Bennett, Jr., and David H. Scott. *Harper's Encyclopedia of Bible Life.* Rev. ed. New York: Harper & Row, 1982.

An illustrated study of daily life in the Biblical era, based on the latest finds.

Thompson, J. A. *Handbook of Life in Bible Times*. Downers Grove, IL: InterVarsity, 1986.

A beautifully illustrated presentation of life in the Biblical era, with maps and charts. Divided into seven parts: I. introductory survey; II. people at home; III. food and drink; IV. industry and commerce; V. culture and health; VI. warfare; VII. religion. Cross-references in margins and selected bibliographies at the end of each chapter. A valuable aid but some inaccuracies occur here and there.

Wright, Fred H. *Manners and Customs of Bible Lands*. Chicago: Moody, 1953.

B. The Social World of the Old Testament

DeVaux, Roland. *Ancient Israel: I. Social Institutions*. New York: McGraw-Hill, 1965.

————— . *Ancient Israel: II. Religious Institutions*. New York: McGraw-Hill, 1965.

Both titles are invaluable studies by a great scholar who for many years lived in Palestine.

Harrison, Roland K. *Old Testament Times*. Grand Rapids, MI: Eerdmans, 1970.

Keel, Othmar. *The Symbolism of the Biblical World*. New York: Seabury, 1978.

Features pictures of statues, symbols, and other discoveries of life in the Biblical period with descriptions of their importance for Biblical study.

Livingston, G. Herbert. *The Pentateuch in Its Cultural Environment*. Grand Rapids, MI: Baker, 1974.

A valuable aid for a better understanding of the Torah.

Pritchard, James B., ed. *The Ancient Near East. I. An Anthology of Text and Pictures*. Princeton, NJ: Princeton University Press, 1958.

————— . *The Ancient Near East: II. A New Anthology of Text and Pictures*. Princeton, NJ: Princeton University Press, 1976.

Both titles shed much light on history, life, and events in the ancient Near East in the Old Testament era. Also available in paperback form.

C. Social World of the New Testament

Barrett, C. K., ed. *New Testament Background: Selected Documents.* New York: Harper & Row, 1961.
A collection of documents illustrating aspects of life and customs of the New Testament era.

Grant, Robert. *Early Christianity and Society.* New York: Harper & Row, 1977.
A collection of seven essays that help to shed light on life in the New Testament era.

Grant, Michael. *Cities of Vesuvius: Pompeii and Herculaneum.* New York: Hamlyn, 1974.
Drawing on the archaeological finds in the two towns destroyed in A.D. 79, Grant provides much information on the total life-pattern.

Judge, E. A. *The Social Pattern of the Christian Groups in the First Century.* London: Tyndale, 1960.
A pioneer resource by a famous classicist.

Kee, Howard C. *The New Testament in Context: Sources and Documents.* Englewood Cliffs, NJ: Prentice-Hall, 1984.
A selection of documents illustrating the religious, social and political structures, and literary conventions of the first century.

Lefkowitz, Mary R., and Maureén B. Fant. *Women's Life in Greece and Rome.* Baltimore: Johns Hopkins University Press, 1982.
A selection of translations from ancient sources on the life of women in ancient Greece and Rome.

Lyall, Francis. *Slaves, Citizens, Sons: Legal Metaphors in the Epistles.* Grand Rapids, MI: Zondervan, 1984.
An authoritative and invaluable resource on legal metaphors used especially by the apostle Paul.

MacMullen, Ramsay. *Paganism in the Roman Empire.* New Haven, CT: Yale University Press, 1981.
Examines major cults from the social and cultural perspective.

Malherbe, Abraham J. *Social Aspects of Early Christianity.* 2nd ed., enlarged. Philadelphia: Fortress, 1983.

Describes social levels and literary culture, house churches and their problems, and hospitality in the church.

Massey, Michael, ed. *Society in Imperial Rome*. New York: Cambridge University Press, 1982.
A selection of translations on life in Rome, dining out, Roman women, and slavery.

Nash, Ronald H. *Christianity and the Hellenistic World*. Grand Rapids, MI: Zondervan, 1984.
A survey of the total context of Christianity.

Stambaugh, John E., and David L. Balch. *The New Testament in Its Social Environment*. Library of Early Christianity. Philadelphia: Westminster, 1986.
A careful study of the historical background, mobility of religions, the ancient economy, society in Palestine, city life, and Christianity in cities of the Roman empire. References to the New Testament treated from the critical viewpoint.

Teringo, J. Robert. *The Land and People Jesus Knew: A Visual Tour of First-Century Palestine*. Minneapolis: Bethany, 1985.
Sketches together with descriptive copy of life in Bible lands by the associate art director of the *National Geographic Magazine*.

Tidball, Derek. *The Social Context of the New Testament: A Sociological Analysis*. Grand Rapids, MI: Zondervan, 1984.
A theological, sociological analysis of the early church and its outreach, the Gentile environment, the social status of early Christians, and the church's relationship to the world.

Wiedemann, Thomas. *Greek and Roman Slavery*. Baltimore: Johns Hopkins University Press, 1981.
A collection of translations from major Greek and Roman writings illustrating every aspect of slavery.